# ANDREE

# AT THE NORTH POLE

WITH

## DETAILS OF HIS FATE

BY

LEON LEWIS

AUTHOR OF "THE SERF LOVERS OF SIBERIA," "THE YOUNG CASTAWAYS," "KIT CARSON'S LAST TRAIL," "THE DIAMOND SEEKER OF BRAZIL," ETC., ETC.

ILLUSTRATED

NEW YORK

G. W. Dillingham Co., Publishers

MDCCCXCIX

R

# INTRODUCTORY.

THE idea of reaching the North Pole in a balloon occurred to Andree in 1882–'83, while he was spending the winter in Spitzbergen as a member of a scientific expedition. This idea grew upon him during years of subsequent toil and study, in the course of which a number of notable aerial voyages gave him the necessary training and experience, especially that of the 19th of October, 1893, when he was carried by a westerly wind across the Baltic to Finland, and that of the 29th of November, 1894, when he was carried three hundred miles across the Baltic from Gothenburg to the Island of Gothland.

During all his voyages and ascensions, the intrepid explorer gave constant attention to the great problem of steering his balloon by guide-ropes and sails, achieving a success in this line which he regarded as full of promise. The usual difficulties, financial included, manifested themselves in his later efforts to make a decisive move northward, but he overcame them all with rare energy, tact and courage, and eventually sailed away, with two worthy associates, from Dane's Island, off the west coast of Spitzbergen, on the 11th of July, 1897.

The daring explorers were three in number, all Swedes, as follows:

SALOMON AUGUST ANDREE,

Dr. NILS STRINDBERG,

KNUT FRAENCKEL.*

Their balloon had been named " ORNEN," " The Eagle." One of its distinctive features was a couple of strong guide-ropes, intended to keep the balloon at a uniform height. They also served as

* Through the courtesy of Mr. Charles K. Johansen, publisher of the Valkyrian, we are enabled to present reproductions of the Life Portraits of our Heroes, photographed in Sweden, by Axel Stake.

a keel to the airship, which was provided with three sails the explorers intended to handle in such a way as to shape their course in accordance with their wishes. The balloon had a capacity of 170,000 cubic feet, and was 67¼ feet in diameter, with a lifting power of 9,000 pounds, or 4½ tons. The belief of Andree and his associates was that the Eagle would lose only 50 cubic feet of gas per day, and hence that it would remain afloat a month. Its basket, or car, was seven feet in diameter and five feet in depth. Above this was the observatory, in which were the sextants, glasses and other instruments, and from which a lookout was habitually kept. A stove was suspended twenty-five feet below the car, and was for cooking only. Ample supplies of food for a number of months had been provided, and the explorers took aboard with them several carrier pigeons and dogs.

These various preparations and the details of events preceding the start having been repeatedly described at length by the newspapers throughout the civilized world, the author of the following narrative has no call to linger upon them, but will

proceed at once to answer the very natural questions arising everywhere as to where the explorers
went and what happened to them, and will plunge
directly into his subject, taking it up at the very
moment of the departure of the brave and devoted
aeronauts upon their ever-memorable journey.*

* The story of " Andree at the North Pole," in almost its
complete form, as now published, originally appeared in the
New York *Evening World.*

# CONTENTS.

## CHAPTER I.

[11]

## CHAPTER VI.

## CHAPTER VII.

## CHAPTER VIII.

## CHAPTER IX.

## CHAPTER X.

## CHAPTER XI.

## CHAPTER XII.

## CHAPTER XIII.

## CHAPTER XIV.

## CHAPTER XV.

## CHAPTER XVI.

## CHAPTER XVII.

## CHAPTER XVIII.

## CHAPTER XIX.

## CHAPTER XX.

## CHAPTER XXI.

## CHAPTER XXII.

## CHAPTER XXIII.

## CHAPTER XXIV.

## CHAPTER XXV.

## CHAPTER XXVI.

## CHAPTER XXVII.

## CHAPTER XXVIII.

## CHAPTER XXIX.

## CHAPTER XXX.

## CHAPTER XXXI.

ANDREE'S BALLOON-HOUSE AT DANES' ISLAND, SPITZBERGEN, FROM WHICH THE START WAS MADE.

# ANDREE AT THE NORTH POLE.

———•———

## CHAPTER I.

*A Surprising Visitant from the Unknown North-
land—Who and What is He, and What His
Motives ?*

" GIF AKT !" cried Andree, as the balloon started
upwards, with a succession of jars and jerks, accompanied by a strange clatter of ropes and a rat-
tling of stones and gravel.

His companions gave all their attention accordingly to the unexpected phenomena which had
startled him. They even held their breath a few
moments, while the shocks and jars continued, and
then a sigh of relief escaped them.

[15]

They had cleared the earth safely, as well as the balloon-house in which the Eagle had been kept and inflated, and were soaring swiftly upwards.

Not a voice disturbed the silence for the next two or three minutes. For Andree himself this start northward was the realization of a dream he had cherished during fourteen years, and his companions, Dr. Strindberg and Knut Fraenckel, were scarcely less delighted than their leader. But all had been rendered anxious by the entanglement of the guide-ropes, which had attended their departure, and could not help waiting and watching to see if any harm had come to the balloon from it.*

"We ought to rise faster than this," were the next words of Andree.

"Surely, after losing half our guide-ropes!" returned Dr. Strindberg.

"Singular!" pursued Andree, scanning the heights behind the balloon-house, where Jonas

---

* A "mishap," Jonas Stadling calls it in his article, "Andree's Flight Into the Unknown," in the *Century Magazine* for November, 1897. As will be seen, I take a different view of the occurrence, ascribing it to the machinations of Pirr Garvel.

Stadling, a warm friend of the explorers, was tak-ing successive photographs of the balloon's pro-gress.* "Can any one have tampered with the balloon?"

' "Or with the guide-ropes?" suggested Fraen-ckel. "It's certainly strange that they should have caught in anything. Has some secret enemy tried to wreck us at the start?"

"If so, they have made a failure of it," declared Andree, with involuntary sternness. "We're doing fairly well, and may regard our start as a success."

Silence reigned again, while the balloon slowly changed its course from northward to north, rising higher and higher every moment, and seeming to resign itself consciously to the current of air bear-ing it between the mountains.

At length Andree drew a sigh of profound relief.

"I was afraid we shouldn't rise fast enough to clear the peaks of Fogelsang," he said, "but we shall. We're up a thousand feet or more already, and still rising."

* Reproduced in the aforesaid article in the *Century*.

"And making good time—not far from thirty miles an hour," announced Fraenckel. "The Pole is ours."

"If the wind will only last," sighed Strindberg.

Little more was said until the peaks of Fogelsang had been left behind the explorers, and unknown vistas were beginning to present themselves ahead of them.

"We seem to be getting on all right," then remarked Andree, a smile illuminating his face for the first time since his departure.

"Yes, we're fairly launched into the unknown, as Stadling is always putting it," returned Strindberg. "The balloon is not as buoyant as it ought to be, but—"

The doctor hesitated, looking startled, as he stared straight ahead, but soon continued:

"What's that thing moving yonder? A mirage of our balloon?"

His companions turned their attention breathlessly in the direction indicated, and were just able to make out through the gray, dull atmosphere some sort of an object, almost like a small cloud, which had come into view from behind a peak.

"A flock of birds," suggested Fraenckel.

"It's a balloon!" gasped the doctor, after a long study of the distant object. "And it's coming toward us!"

"An aerial craft of some kind, sure," confirmed Andree, with the air of being unable to fully credit his senses. "And it's coming to meet us—in the teeth of the wind!"

A tremor of wonder and apprehension shook them. Was the strange air-ship coming to make war upon them?

"She's moving like lightning!" exclaimed Fraenckel.

It was true! The three explorers had barely time to recover a portion of their self-possession when the aerial craft rounded to alongside The Eagle, shutting off steam from its propellers, and began to drift northward with them.

What they saw startled them.

A cigar-shaped hull, some forty feet in length by eight or ten feet in diameter, and surmounted by

two immense screws of aluminum of three or four
turns, and the largest at the top, with funicular
paddle-wheels on each side of the hull and steering
contrivances at each end—these were the salient
features of the mysterious aerial crusier.

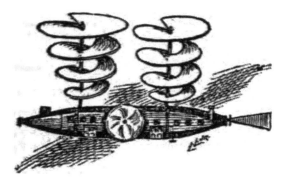

A solitary passenger stood at the top of one end
of the cigar-shaped hull, in a sort of cage, from
which he directed the craft's movements.

"You've started, I see," observed this man, in
excellent English, bowing and smiling.

Andree assented dumbly, unable to speak, realizing that this man had possessed some foreknowledge of his intentions.

"It's a pity you've only such a tub as that for
your explorations," pursued the stranger, surveying

The Eagle with undisguised scorn and contempt.
"You are in a fair way to give your lives for nothing."

"Who are you?" asked Andree, with an abrupt-
ness born of his surprise, which was too great to be
mastered.

"My name is Pirr Garvel," was the answer.

"Where are you from, Mr. Garvel?"

"From the other side of those hills," answered
the stranger, with a careless gesture to the northward. "I was coming to see you, Herr Andree."

"Ah! You know who—who we are?" stam-
mered the explorer.

"Yes, and what you are doing—or what you are
trying to do," he added with a singular smile.

"And you were coming to see us?"

"Yes, incidentally, having business the other
side of Spitzbergen. I had decided to counsel you
against starting on this ill-advised expedition."

"Indeed," returned Andree, looking his wonder.
"You're too late for that. Besides, you're 'counsel' wouldn't have stopped us."

"Well, no harm's done," continued the solitary

aerian, his smile deepening. "You will get a little bit of experience which may be of some use in the future. Good-by. I'll see you again about day after to-morrow."

"And why ' about day after to-morrow?'" demanded Andree.

"Oh, this wind is not going to last," announced the stranger, in the same easy and careless tone which had characterized all his previous utterances. "You will be going in the opposite direction in a few hours—certainly before morning. *Au revoir, messieurs.*"

He touched an ivory handle lightly and the funicular wheels on the side of the cigar-shaped hull began revolving, as the aluminum screw above the strange craft had not ceased to do since its arrival. Sheering off and making a half turn, the mysterious aerial cruiser was soon moving southward, directly against the wind, at a rate of speed exceeding half a mile a minute.

"Well, I declare!" was the ejaculation of supreme astonishment that escaped Andree when he

could speak.   " What is he, this Pirr Garvel—man
or demon ?"

Well might he ask.   Here was a man, speaking
both English and French and dwelling somewhere
in an unknown northland, who had solved the problem of aerial navigation.

" And evidently he has been watching us and
keeping himself informed of our project and proceedings," muttered Fraenckel.   " To what end
and purpose ?   In what way is he interested ?   And
why was he coming to ' counsel ' us ?"

## CHAPTER II.

*Andree Gives His Associates Various Reasons for Believing in the Existence of a Highly Civilized Nation at the North Pole—Startling Confirmation of This View by a Mirage.*

THE silence that succeeded these comments upon Pirr Garvel was not merely one of wonder, but also of consternation and disgust. It was no pleasant experience for the explorers, after years of trials and struggles, to see this mysterious stranger carrying off the honors of the occasion in such a light and airy fashion.

" Evidently we are little more than untutored savages in comparison with this magician from the Unknown," at length growled Andree. " Who and what can he be !"

The doctor smiled sarcastically.

" He is our master and superior—that's clear enough," he declared ; " but he's neither English nor

American, although he speaks the language like a native. His face is a singular one—as clear-cut as that of a devil, and as wicked. One would say he's of a new and unknown race."

"I think I can place him," said Andree thoughtfully. "He's a native of the country for which we have started, and hence his interest in us."

"That sounds reasonable," commented the doctor. "But I'm afraid his interest in us is not altogether friendly or disinterested."

"Perhaps not," returned Fraenckel; "but it's clear that he's not our enemy, since it would cost him no more to wipe us out than to snuff a candle. His name tells us little—as odd as it is—but his steam-balloon, or air-steamer, whatever we may call it, and the ease with which he handles it, tells us a great deal."

"Just what does it tell us?" queried Andree. "Define that point."

"Why, it tells us that he belongs to a people vastly superior to our own in science and progress," declared Fraenckel, without a moment's hesitation.

"That craft of his realizes what we have only dreamed."

"True," admitted Andree, "but there's a reason for his superiority. He belongs to a far older nation than ours. As I said, I think I can place him. Did it ever occur to you why all the great nations of the earth have made such persistent efforts during hundreds of years to reach the North Pole?"

"Because they wanted to see what was there," replied Fraenckel, smiling.

"Or to take possession," suggested Strindberg.

"That's true, but not the whole truth," pursued Andree. "The great powers have been drawn into these explorations by a psychic influence they themselves have not fully comprehended. In a word, they have been drawn into these efforts and sacrifices by the fact that there is a branch of the human family, a sister nation, at the North Pole."

"Esquimaux?" queried Fraenckel.

"No," returned Andree; "a people as far removed from the Esquimaux as possible."

"Men in the style of Garvel, then?"

"Yes, a nation of Garvels. Do you remember

Captain Symmes's book, 'The Hollow Globe,' in which he claims that there is an opening into the earth at the North Pole ?"

His companions assented.

"Well," continued Andree, "Captain Symmes was mistaken. There's no such opening into the interior of the earth, as he supposed. But it's a fact that there is a natural depression at each pole—a great basin, a hollow, so to speak—the polar dia-meter of the earth being twenty-six miles less than the equatorial ; and the climate of this vast basin has always been supposed to be a mild one. Do you recall what Kane and others have said about ' an open polar sea ?' "

" Assuredly," answered Fraenckel.

" Well, I believe not merely in the existence of that ' open polar sea,' " declared Andree, " but also in the existence of a great polar continent, or of an island worthy of being called a continent. To be sure, there exists at the rim of the great natural depression of which I have spoken an ' icy barrier ' or ' polar pack,' which has always been the terror of navigators, and which is responsible for the no-

tion that the cold increases with every step northward. But this notion is incorrect—absolutely
erroneous.  Once we have passed this 'icy barrier,'
we shall reach a mild climate, a country of wood
and water, a wilderness of verdure and vegetation,
the dwelling-place of bird, beast and fowl—in short,
a habitable and inhabited country, in all the best
conditions and meanings of the term."

"You think so ?" demanded Fraenckel.

"I know it," asserted Andree, with a seriousness
approaching solemnity.  "To begin with, the existence of the 'open polar sea' has been proved by
the passage of schools of whales through it from
the waters of Greenland to those of Behring
Sea——"

"And especially by the voyage made by the
famous oilskin garment thrown overboard from the
Jeannette," interrupted Strindberg.

"Exactly ; and by many other facts and circumstances, into which I needn't enter," continued the
explorer.  "The object of our voyage, therefore,
is not to reach an icy desert, indicated on our maps
by a blank space and labelled 'North Pole,' but to

find that important branch of our race, that sister nation, or 'lost' people, which has been existing in the great basin of the North Pole from time immemorial.   Did you ever read a book called ' The Molten Globe?"

" I did.  It was written by Mr. Green, who was Premier of the Hawaiian Islands at the time.   I bought a copy of the publisher, Mr. Sanford, of Charing Cross, London."

" And what do you think of it ?"

" Why, I think he proves his contention, namely that the earth was once in a molten condition, after first being gaseous, and that these facts are fully proven by its shape and features."

" That's all perfectly true," declared Andree. " Did you ever read a book in which it is claimed that the North Pole was the cradle of our race?"

Strindberg assented, giving author and title.

"Well, the arguments of that book have never been controverted," continued Andree.  " These authors show how the earth, formerly a molten mass, first became habitable at the North Pole by due process of cooling, and the latter claims that it is at the North Pole that we must look for the mysterious 'Garden of Eden' of the theologians. Be that as it may, I have no hesitation in saying that the great mother-nation of the Aryans sent forth her colonies from that quarter."

"The Aryans?" repeated Fraenckel, with an air of imperfect comprehension.

"Yes, the Aryans," explained Andree; "the oldest nation which has left a name in human annals; the mother of all existing races; the source from which has come every civilized being upon our planet."

"Is this a certainty?" asked Strindberg.

"Absolutely," replied Andree. "See 'Aryans,' in any good encyclopedia.* And, since I have no

* See also, Who are the Aryans? by Prof. John Fiske, in the *Atlantic* Monthly, Feb., 1881, who explains "in what sense we may all properly be called Aryans." He says: The Aryana of the present day is much more than an Indo-European region. Its eastern boundaries have altered but little for many centuries; but on the west it has extended to the Pacific coast of America, and on the other side of the world it has begun to annex territory in South Africa and Australia. Indeed, if we are to judge from what has been going on since the times of Drake and Frobisher, it seems in every way likely that men of English speech will by and by have

doubt of the occupancy of the North Pole count-
less thousands of years ago by the primitive Aryans,
I cannot hesitate to believe that we shall find there
a people descended directly from them."

"What sort of a people?" inquired Fraenckel.

"Possibly a people like the primitive Aryans,
and which may be best described as one possessing
all the virtues of civilization and none of its vices,"
answered Andree. "The primitive Aryans were
tillers of the soil with fixed abodes, and possessed
every sort of virtue and wisdom, every degree of
household developement and civic honor, all the
ties of family and friendship, and every sort of use-
fulness, culture and comfort."

"How do we know this?" asked Fraenckel.

"From the fact that they had words in their language for all those ties of family and moral qualities which are ours, and that those words have come
down to us in all the modern tongues of Europe
and Asia."

seized upon every part of the earth's surface not already covered by a well-established civilization, and will have converted
them all into Aryan countries."

"And what of the dark side of life—war, blood-shed and so on?" demanded Strindberg.

"They didn't so much as have words for such things in their language," assured Andree. "From what we know of the every-day life of those primi-tive Aryans we cannot doubt that it presented, during thousands of years, a picture worthy of Eden."

A more desolate scene than that which now lay spread out beneath the daring explorers cannot possibly be imagined.

Far as the eye could reach in any direction were immense plains of snow and ice, with here and there a patch of open water or a mountain peak, many of the latter resembling pinnacles and towers, and presenting all sorts of fantastic shapes and com-binations.

For a long time—or until six o'clock—hardly another remark disturbed the silence, so intense was the interest of the explorers in the succession of views presented to them.

But suddenly, as they turned their gaze anew in

the direction they were going, a cry of surprise burst from them.

Far up toward the Pole and low on the horizon —in such a situation, in fact, that it had been eclipsed by the balloon-basket—a radiant city, re-

markably rich in temples and towers, had taken form and color across the face of the heavens."

"Am I dreaming?" gasped Fraenckel, "or is it reality?"

"It's a reality," affirmed Andree, with clasped

hands and a countenance glowing with ineffable joy. "It's a mirage of that great Shadowy City of the Pole, which has been seen repeatedly in the Western Hemisphere, and which has been pictured in the American newspapers!"

"May it not be a mirage of St. Petersburg, Christania, Stockholm or Quebec?" asked Fraenckel.

"No, or we should recognize some of its leading features," responded Andree. "It's a projection from the Unknown we have invaded, and resembles nothing in Europe or America!"

"Yet it represents a city that actually exists?" queried the doctor.

"Of course it does—that glorious city of the Pole we are out to discover.'

For a few minutes the trio stood in wondering ecstasy, as lurid lights and tremulous shadows commingled and danced across the walls and pinnacles of the gigantic spectral city, suspended in the sky ahead of them, and then a sigh, which was also a cry of amazement, escaped them.

The phantom city had vanished!

"Yes, there is a great city and people somewhere in the unknown regions ahead of us," declared Andree, with an air of absolute certainty.
"On no other theory can we account for the startling sight we have just witnessed—or for our visit
from Pirr Garvel!"

He glanced anew at the various features of the
scene in which he was figuring, and added :

"We shall gain nothing by remaining on the
*qui vive* here.   Let's shut ourselves up in the basket
and have a bite.   I was too busy and excited to-
day to get outside of my dinner."

The suggestion was duly acted upon, the trio
accompanying their lunch with a renewed discussion of their plans and prospects, while the balloon
continued its steady flight northward.

## CHAPTER III.

*Blown Back Across Spitzbergen—An Event More
Exciting than Crusoe's Discovery of the Foot-
print in the Sand.*

A FEW minutes after finishing their supper the
explorers discovered that the wind had become
light and variable, and a shadow of regret and con-
cern gathered upon their features.

'Nevertheless, we must take things as we find
them," suggested Andree, after a brief discussion
of the situation. " My idea is not to fret at anything that may happen, or even at the worst that
can happen."

" Mine also," avowed Fraenckel.

" Furthermore," said Strindberg, " I do not intend to kill myself with useless labor, such as trying
to make this balloon go north when the wind is
blowing in the opposite direction. My idea is to
reserve our strength for those moments and occasions when it can be expended to advantage."

KNUT FRÆNCKEL.

" I was about to make a suggestion to that effect," said FraenckeL " There's no telling how soon we may be called upon to use all our strength and endurance, and for that reason we must battle with the unnecessary as little as possible. I think one of us, for example, can take just as good care of this ship as all three of us, and in consequence of that conviction I suggest that the sooner two of us turn in for a good nap the better."

" You and the Doctor shall be the first to have the benefit of this reasoning," decided Andree instantly. " As a simple matter of fact, I am too excited to sleep—too full of speculations concerning our future and what fate has in store for us."

Left in charge, Andree raised his head out of the basket of his observatory, the rim of which sustained his elbow—took possession of his " lookout," in fact—and turned his attention within and without as only a man can when he has taken his life in his hands in the execution of some inexorable purpose.

" It remains to be seen whether I have been a wise man or a fool," ran his musings. " If I had been blessed with a wife, as Nansen is—if there had been even one life indissolubly associated with mine—why, I never should have started upon this journey, should never have dared to face the terrible risks and perils which await us. As it is, what does it matter? Life, at the best, is a fleeting dream, and few there are who get through with it without many a rude awakening."

For hours he stood there, attentive to everything around him, noting the progress he was making, and watching the fluctuations of the uncertain wind that was bearing him onward.

" Things are going from bad to worse," at length escaped him. " The wind has shifted to the north, as Pirr Garvel said it would, and we shall be driven back to Dane's Island !"

This conviction was such torture that he hastened to arouse his companions.

Despite all their philosophy, latent and expressed, the next few hours were spent by the explorers in fretting and chafing against the adverse wind which had assailed them. Early in the new day * they

* The day referred to here is the astronomical day of twenty-four hours.

NILS STRINDBERG.

recognized several peaks at the north end of Spitzbergen, and realized that they were being borne
slowly to the eastward and southward of the point
from which they had started.  In fact, when the
sun had reached its lowest declension again they
were in a fair way to be blown, in a southeasterly
direction, clear across the island.

We need not linger upon the events of the long
hours that succeeded, or upon those of the following morning, the light of which showed them that
they were drifting before a northwest wind over
the Arctic Ocean and out of sight of land.

"At this rate we're far more likely to fetch up in
Norway than at the North Pole," declared Andree
with undisguised bitterness.

"Patience!" enjoined Strindberg.  "The wind
may veer to the south at any moment."

The day wore on, bringing a few distractions,
such as taking the latitude and longitude and send-
ing out another pigeon.*  About the middle of

* With this message: July 13, 12.30 P. M.   Latitude 82.2 ;
longitude 15.5 East.   Good voyage toward the east; ten

the afternoon the situation of the explorers had become so monotonous and wearisome that Andree proposed the reading of some interesting papers he had brought with him.

"They will at least suggest that we are not the first explorers who have had a hard time of it," he declared; "Ah!"

The speaker leaped to his feet excitedly, looking as if he had seen an apparition.

"Did you hear that?" he questioned.

"Hear what?" demanded his companions in chorus.

"A human voice—out here in mid-ocean. "Listen!"

The trio listened accordingly, suspending their respiration, when suddenly out of the wild solitudes beneath them came the piercing screams of a woman, followed by the words:

"Help! help!"

"I scent that Pirr Garvel," muttered Fraenckel.

In an instant Andree was looking over the rim

degrees to the south. All well on board. This is the third pigeon sent out.

of the observatory, even as that agonized cry for help was repeated.

"My God! see there!" escaped him, in a tone of the most intense wonder and excitement.

## CHAPTER IV.

*A New York Girl's Terrible Situation—Andree to
the Rescue.*

THE wreck of a large sailing-ship, dismantled
and water-logged, drifting slowly to the northeast,
her bow pitching forward until it was almost awash
—such was the first object that caught the explorer's attention.

Upon the forward deck of this craft stood a
beautiful girl of some twenty summers, her hands
clasped as if in prayer and her gaze riveted implor-
ingly upon the balloon and its occupants.

" Save me! save me!" she cried, her voice finding new strength at sight of the kindly faces looking down upon her.

It is needless to say how deeply this appeal
stirred the souls of Andree and his companions.

Who could she be? And how had she come
there, so far in the extreme north, amid the ice-

floes of Spitzbergen?  And how could they come
to her relief—how save her?

For a few moments, as was natural, the three
explorers stared at one another in blank helplessness, pity and horror.

Then they noticed that the balloon, now at a
height of twelve or thirteen hundred feet, was
almost becalmed, the wind from the north having
died out and no new one having definitely set in.
They saw, too, by such motion as The Eagle possessed that it was likely to drift over the wreck
or very near it, and in this fact appeared a first
ray of hope.

"Perhaps something can be done," suggested
the doctor.  "We might at least keep the poor
girl company.  Would it not be wise, as things
have turned out, to open the valve and take refuge
on the wreck, abandoning the balloon?  To do
this may be our last chance of ever seeing old
Sweden."

The temptation to act upon this suggestion was
certainly a strong one.  Again and again during
their two days in the air, and especially since

finding themselves adrift over the ocean, the trio had discussed the probability—nay, certainty—of encountering watery graves if the balloon should burst or suddenly lose its buoyancy. But Andree shook his head emphatically.

"That would be out of the frying-pan into the fire," he declared. "I'd sooner take my chances here than there. Just notice how low the wreck is down by the head! She may be near her final plunge."

"Besides, the young woman may be out of provisions," said Fraenckel. "Her situation must be desperate indeed, if she can see in our presence any promise of relief!"

"And such it is no doubt," rejoined Andree, as the girl raised her clasped hands beseechingly above her head. "All that keeps the wreck afloat is the lumber with which she is laden. What can we do?"

"There is just one opening for us—since we are drifting across the course the wreck is taking," advised Strindberg, after another rapid glance around and below. "Knut and I must remain afloat, while you descend to the wreck!"

"If the thing's possible," breathed Fiaenckel, with suppressed excitement.

"Quick, then—get hold of that ballast-line," requested Andree, after watching the intersecting courses of the ship and the balloon for a few moments. "There appears to be a chance for us to make connections—yes, a good one! At the worst, I shall have only a cold bath and a short swim! Lively!"

He passed a light anchor over the side of the basket, while his associates laid hold of the stout rope which had been made fast to the instrument during the day for any such emergency, and in another moment he was being lowered rapidly, his feet resting in the hollows of the flukes.

A wilder, more terrible spectacle has never been seen than that he presented a few minutes later, swinging and swaying in the air at the end of four hundred yards of rope, and suspended between sky and ocean like a spider between floor and ceiling!

"Faster! Pay out the line faster!" suddenly cried the explorer in a startled voice.

His companions com-plied.

"There! Hold fast!" he soon added, with a change of voice from alarm to triumph. "It's done!"

Such was indeed the case! So well had every-thing been timed and combined that the dar-

ing aeronaut had reached the deck of the ship at just the right moment to pass the end of his ballast-line around the rail of the bulwarks, and key it with a fluke of the anchor, thus making the balloon fast to the wreck.

"Oh! I was so afraid you would plunge into the water—which is full of sharks," faltered the girl, moving toward him with tottering steps and pallid countenance, as if barely able to retain her senses and powers of locomotion.

"I saw them, and for a few moments thought my time had come," returned Andree, inclining his hardy, commanding figure politely and hastening to meet her.

"I'm so glad they didn't get you—so glad you've come to me," she continued, extending a hand of the most exquisite contours. "What joy! what relief!"

Andree wrung her hand, rather than shook it, his soul in a tumult at the strangeness of his situation, in connection with the charm of such a radiant presence, her awful peril and his terrifying surroundings.

"Your joy and relief are mine," he responded, his gaze lingering upon her in exultant surprise and admiring rapture.

"And to think of your coming to me in such a manner and through such perils!" cried the girl wildly, wringing her hands unconsciously, her sweet face paling and flushing, her eyes glowing, her lips tremulous with feeling. "To see you here at such a moment, after days and weeks of this horrible and lonely life in this foundering wreck."

She finished with a suppressed scream of terror, the ship having given a long, staggering pitch forward, as if it would disappear forever.

"And to think of your strange arrival here," she resumed, as she tottered nearer, grasping his arm, and looking with wild deliciousness of hope and relief into the noble countenance before her—"your coming here at such a time, when the fire is out and we have no matches to relight it, when our provisions are exhausted, when poor papa is ill almost unto death, when both of us are so cold and hungry, and when the very shadow of death seems to be de-

scending upon us. Oh, heaven has indeed heard
our prayers ; heaven has indeed been merciful !"

The frame of the strong man beside her shook
under these impassioned outpourings of the girl's
agonized soul like the leaves of an aspen.

It was in vain that his reason whispered that he
might have come there only to die with her, or
within a few hours later. Not for worlds would he
have failed to find consolation for that sorely tried
girl, as she thus clung to him, her soul in her gaze,
her heart torn and rent by a flood of griefs and
apprehensions.

"That's right," he responded, with the gentle
earnestness the occasion demanded. " Do not doubt
that relief is at hand and that heaven has sent me
to you. Do not fear—do not worry. Be calm and
hopeful. I will save you !"

He flung a resolute glance into the lowering
heavens and the still wilder waters, and made a gesture to his comrades, who hastened to act upon it.

" Patience !" he breathed, turning anew to the
girl. " We'll soon see our way out of this."

Another long plunge of the wreck, with a swish.

ing of water beneath the deck, sent his glance upward again, and then he demanded, with a half-
defined purpose of withdrawing the girl's attention
from their perils :

" Are you not an American ?"

" Yes," she answered. " I am from New York,
where papa is a clergyman. I am his only daughter, Alice Haddon."

" I am so glad to meet you, Miss Haddon—so
glad, despite all your perils and mine, and perhaps
because of them," returned Andree, his earnest,
honest face a picture of the tenderest respect and
admiration. " Perhaps you have heard of me during the years I have been trying to start for the
North Pole. I am Andree, the explorer."

Alice Haddon recoiled two or three steps, with
a cry of interest and gladness, her mood and aspect
changing as if by magic, her eyes losing their wild
and terrorized look, and an intense flash of hope
and relief breaking over her beautiful features.

" Oh, is it possible ?" she cried, " Is it possible
that I thus meet one whose career I have so long
followed and admired ? And one of whom poor

papa and I have so often spoken during the long
and dark nights of this awful voyage ?   This is delightful!"

She looked him over with the brightest of eyes
and rosiest of cheeks, her lips parting in a smile of
gladdest welcome, as if his presence had stirred her
young blood as it had never been stirred before.

" To be honest and candid," she resumed, " papa
and I have talked about you so much during the
last few weeks that you really seem like an old acquaintance."

"I wish I might be accounted such," he responded,
his glances caressing her shyly, with honest daring.
" A strange, wild meeting is ours, Miss Haddon, is
it not?   Well, it's not half so strange and wild as
joyous—for me, I mean."

He hesitated a moment, with a glance at his surroundings, including the sharks whose jaws he had
so narrowly escaped, and then, as if life were too
full of peril, too uncertain to require the suppres-
sion of the love and tenderness which invaded his
soul, he frankly added ;

"I should have missed the one great gladness of my life if I hadn't met you."

"And I, too," she answered.

There was no need of saying more at that perilous moment. They realized that they had met for all eternity—that eye had spoken unto eye, and that heart was calling unto heart. Aye, they knew then and there that existence had become a supreme gladness for both, even if they were fated to die together!

## CHAPTER V.

*Pirr Garvel a Menace and a Terror—The Explorers again in Peril.*

ANOTHER long, staggering pitch of the wreck aroused the couple from the thrill of bliss which had rendered them oblivious for one brief moment to their dreadful situation.

" And to think that I came near shutting myself up in the cabin and saying nothing to you, Mr. Andree !" exclaimed Alice.

" That would have been a great mistake," he responded.

" It would, indeed !   Only death could have been the outcome of such an error."

" But why should you even think of such a thing as hiding ?" he asked.

" I was afraid," she answered, " that you might have some connection with an odious stranger who has intruded upon me almost every day for a fortnight."

"How intruded? From where?"

"From the sky—in an airship, only one very different from your balloon."

"What! Pirr Garvel!" Andree could not help suspecting.

"Yes, Pirr Garvel—the Polar Devil, papa calls him. Do you know him?"

"I've seen him," avowed the explorer, with an anxiety even greater than his astonishment. "When was he here last?"

"Yesterday afternoon," replied Alice. "He has fallen in love with me and threatens me with all sorts of vengeance if I do not accept his offer of marriage."

"The monster! What does he tell you about himself?"

"Nothing whatever. He comes and goes like some demon of the air."

"Has he given you no information about his home, country or people?"

Alice shook her head.

"Has he betrayed anything about his kindred or

dwelling-place, in the course of his dealings with you ?"

"Not a thing, except that he lives somewhere to the northward, the quarter from which he comes and into which he vanishes, so far as we have had opportunities of noting his comings and goings."

"And does he know how you are situated here, lacking fuel and fire, out of food and in danger of being engulfed in the ocean at any moment ?"

"Oh, yes ; he knows it."

"And yet offers no relief ?"

"Only on condition of receiving my promise to marry him.   He came very near setting fire to the wreck and carrying me off yesterday, but finally concluded the wreck would float another day or two, and said he'd come for me after getting rid of another party he has been watching."

"Ah ! I wonder if I am that other party, and if he's searching for me now ?" cried the explorer, again glancing up at his companions and making another energetic gesture, "When did you first see him ?"

"Two weeks ago to-day, when the wreck was five

or six degrees south of here," replied Alice, grasping the explorer's arm, as if the very recollection
of the intruder's advent filled her with terror.
"He berthed his airship upon our deck as easily
as you can place one hand over the other. Oh,
how I fear him! I've never encountered a man
like him—one so cruel and heartless, so daring and
unscrupulous, so knowing and powerful, so utterly
fiendish!"

"But he indicated, didn't he, that he would return for you to-day?" asked the explorer, "May
he not be back shortly?"

"Oh, yes. He may return at any moment. But
what are your people in the balloon doing?"

The explorer looked up, noting that his associates, with the aid of a winch in the balloon basket,
had hauled in the ballast line to such an extent
that The Eagle was now within a dozen yards of
the wreck, tugging gently at the rope that held it
captive.

"They are simply coming to your relief, as I
have directed," explained Andree, his face lighting
up vividly at the prospect of rescuing the girl from

her tormentor. "Things are in bad shape here doubtless."

"Yes, and getting worse every moment."

She waved her hand over the wild waste of waters, dotted here and there with icebergs and fields of ice, in the midst of which a large school of whales was sporting, and added :

"Those sharks have been hanging around the wreck a number of days, as if to announce that they will eventually get us."

" How long have you been adrift in this wreck ?"

" Some six or seven weeks : I know not just how long. We were on our way to Europe when a hurricane struck us. The captain and crew deserted the wreck, thinking it was going down, and didn't even notify papa and me, who were ill in our staterooms. Since then we've drifted and drifted, wondering what would be the end."

" At the best, another week or two of this northward drifting would bring you to a wall of ice, the ' Polar Pack,' even if the wreck should remain afloat so long," said Andree. " What's more, very little wind and sea would be required to send you to the bottom."

"And not a single sail has met our gaze during the six or seven weeks we've been adrift," said Alice. "You can imagine, therefore, how little we dared hope that anyone would come between us and Pirr Garvel."

"You are speaking of 'us' all the time," said Andree. "Where is your father?"

"He's asleep in the cabin. He fell asleep an hour ago, after being awake three or four nights and I had no heart to disturb him. Haven't I told you this? Well, I never!"

She blushed rosily in her confusion, hastily adding:

"Let me take you to him. He will be as delighted as I am. Ah, here he comes."

A man of middle age, of clerical aspect, had indeed made his appearance at the head of the companion-way, looking out upon the young couple with an approving smile.

"Your scream aroused me, daughter, and I have heard and seen everything," he said, advancing to meet them. "Welcome, Mr. Andree; thrice welcome to our floating prison."

He shook hands with the explorer, continuing:

"I doubt not that the Great Hand which guides all human destinies has sent you here to save us."

"And the sooner we leave the wreck the better," suggested Andree, holding up his hand to a sudden puff of wind from the south. "Of course, we must cast off from the wreck as soon as anything like a breeze reaches us, or the balloon would be torn in pieces."

"And it looks now as if we can count upon a favorable breeze," returned the clergyman.

"Perhaps one that will take us to latitude ninety," remarked Andree.

"In any case, Mr. Haddon," resumed Andree, "my associates and I must resume our voyage, and you and Miss Alice had better join us."

"A thousand thanks—we'll do so," said Mr. Haddon. "There are a few things we would like to take with us, but we've already packed them in a small valise, so that we needn't delay our departure but a moment."

"Come, then," returned Andree, with a glance upward at the movements of the balloon. "We'll be off at once, and thus add to our chances of keeping clear of Pirr Garvel."

The father and daughter easily gained their new refuge, with the aid of a rope ladder passed down to them by Fraenckel, and Andree, judging that the wind was favorable and gathering strength from moment to moment, decided to cast off and follow them.

"There's only this one course open to us," he remarked with another glance upward. "If we delay "——

He was strangely, terribly interrupted.

With the quickness of a flash a huge head and crested neck emerged from the depths of the ocean, followed by a round and gleaming body, nearly as large as a barrel and scores of feet in length, taking two turns with marvellous rapidity around one of the largest of the whales which had been spouting near the wreck.

It was in vain that the victim writhed and struggled, lashing the water with its powerful tail.

It was dragged down, down! Its ribs cracked
with reports resembling a rifle's, and in a few moments the waves had closed over it and its assail-
ant.

" And yet the world is full of people who tell us
there is no such thing as a sea serpent," observed
Andree, as he began ascending his rope ladder,
while The Eagle moved briskly upward and northward under the impulse of the new breeze.   " But
we know better !"

A short climb took him safely to the basket,
from which, at the end of a few minutes, he saw
the wreck disappear beneath the waves behind him.
The Haddons had barely made good their escape!

" How long is this balloon expected to remain
afloat?" asked the Rev. Mr. Haddon, after a
thoughtful silence.

" About a month," was the answer.

 · " And for how long are you provisioned ?"

" For some two or three months, according to
our number."

" What have we here with us ?"

Andree replied at some length, making especial

mention of his pigeons and indicating the measures
he would take for the comfort of his passengers.

"When did you start?"

The explorer told him, giving the details known
to the reader.

"It was an adverse wind then that brought you
to the wreck?"

"Exactly."

"Well, sir, it was a very favorable wind for my
daughter and me," declared Mr. Haddon. "Had
it not been for your timely arrival at the wreck
where would Alice and I be at this moment?"

"Where, indeed?"

"Strange mercy of God," breathed the good
man prayerfully. "I shall never cease to thank
Him for bringing us together."

"Nor shall I," returned Andree, his eyes turning
caressingly again to the sweet, joyous face of Alice,
who had already become more to him than all else
in the world.

But suddenly he started as if shot, peering over
the rim of the basket,

"Ah, the wind!" he ejaculated. "It has left us!"

Every eye responded to his with glances of horror.

"And there comes a squall from the east. Hold fast!"

The balloon leaned over abruptly as if about to collapse upon the basket and its occupants, and began dropping rapidly, borne down by the vortex of the gust which had struck it.

Then a profound calm succeeded, lasting two or three minutes and filling the explorers with the wildest anxiety, and it was followed by a breeze which set in from the northwest, carrying the balloon in the opposite direction.

"Heaven help us," prayed Mr. Haddon, dropping upon his knees with clasped hands. "The balloon is still going down and we are being borne out further and further into the ocean!"

## CHAPTER VI.

*Further Discussion by the Explorers of Their Situa-
tion and Prospects.*

FOR two or three minutes Andree hardly
breathed, watching every feature of the situation
as a man caught in a frog might watch an approaching train, and then his brow cleared as suddenly as
it had clouded.

"She rises! she rises!" he announced joyously.
"Once or twice I have seen that phenomenon before, but not so bad as this time. The depression
of the balloon comes from our being caught in a
descending vortex of the squall. There, it has
passed!"

"Thank God, we are safe!" murmured Alice.
"See, the wind has got back to the south again!"

"Yes, we are all right now," returned the explorer. "I have often noticed in these latitudes that
a change of wind is accompanied by these passing

disturbances. Be calm, all; be calm. As things look now the danger is past. The balloon is not only rising to our former level, but she begins to pull in the desired direction."

These views were fully sustained by the events of the next quarter of an hour, the breeze blowing steadily and freshly from the south, and The Eagle taking the course her passengers were anxious to follow.

On and on she flew, and it would have been easy to see that the fine progress they were soon making had a vastly exhilarating effect upon the spirits of the explorers. This was especially true of Andree and Mr. Haddon.

"For a few moments I was scared, thinking the extra load furnished by Alice and myself was carrying us down to certain destruction in the waves," exclaimed the latter. "But she seems to have the lifting power necessary for getting away with us."

"Oh, yes; she's all right now," returned the explorer. "Her lifting power is from four to five tons. In case of need we can 'lighten ship' by throwing out ballast and plenty of objects equivalent to ballast.   As you see, however, we seem to be getting on finely."

" How fast are we moving?"

" Oh, some twelve miles an hour."

" Not more?"

" Hardly.   The fact is, the new breeze has not fully set in."

" About how far from the North Pole are we?"

" Between four and five hundred miles—say, four hundred and fifty."

" Just what is our course at this moment?"

" As near north as may be."

"Oh, if we could only keep this up," exclaimed Alice, her cheeks glowing with enthusiasm.

" That is the point; if we could only keep this up," returned Andree.

" Have you really started out, Mr. Andree, with the intention of reaching the North Pole?" demanded the clergyman.

" With the 'intention'— no.   Merely with the hope of reaching it, and that hope is hardly an expectation, and still less a probability.   We have simply started out to make such an examination of the North Polar regions as wind and weather will permit us to accomplish. All you have seen in print about my 'proposed journey to the North Pole,' or 'Andree's voyage to the North Pole,' is merely the popular way of expressing the world's view of the matter. Needless to add, that a man cannot fix his destination beforehand when he embarks on this sort of machine, but must go where he is carried, drifted or driven."

" But a couple of days with favoring winds would take us to the Pole, wouldn't they ?"

" Sure, if the direction of these winds remained substantially as at present," affirmed Andree. " But can we count upon any such breeze or succession of breezes ?   I have seen too much of aerial navigation to undertake to forecast either wind or weather, especially in these high latitudes."

" I have long been interested in polar explorations," pursued the clergyman, "and have given especial attention, Mr. Andree, to all you have been saying and doing.  Do you believe there are people living at the North Pole ?"

" Not necessarily at that exact point," replied

Andree, "for the simple reason that an open sea may occupy it. With this proviso, I will answer your query in the affirmative. I have no doubt whatever—not the slightest—that the great Polar Basin has its own distinctive inhabitants, and in all probability its own races and nations."

"I believe so, too, and shall never doubt it until our explorers have shown to the contrary," declared the clergyman. "The first condition of such occupancy is, of course, a mild climate and a soil capable of producing food, but I believe a single day's journey in the direction we are going and at our present rate of speed would land us in the midst of scores of proofs of that mildness which could not be disputed."

"That view is also mine, sir," avowed Andree, "and hence you will comprehend the eagerness and resolution with which I have entered upon this voyage. Those polar natives really exist, and it will not be my fault if they fail to present themselves to our observation—not merely in isolated specimens, like Garvel, but as a people."

"Do you regard the North Pole as one of the

ancient dwelling-places of our race, Mr. Andree?" inquired Alice.

"Yes, as one of the oldest, if not the most ancient of all," answered the explorer. "Astronomy and geology, climate and geography all point in that direction."

"But will these people necessarily be like us?" continued the girl, her gaze lingering upon the features of her rescuer with restful contentment.

"Like us as far as type is concerned," answered Andree, "but they may be in many ways our superiors. For instance, they may live hundreds of years, and derive their nourishment from the earth or air. It is already known to medical men that the human heart is a dynamo—purely and simply a dynamo—and that human life is either a form of electricity or the product of electricity, and it is not too much to claim, even at this early stage of our knowledge, that the food of our race will some day be served up in a purer and more etherealized form. It is further known that the geographical axis of our globe is also its electrical axis, and hence we may assume that the native of the North

Pole will be a sort of electrical man, or walking Leyden jar, of which a hint has been given us in various electrical eels and fishes."

Alice stirred uneasily, as if a new and strange light had suddenly dawned upon her.

" Why, that theory would account for the influence of Pirr Garvel upon me whenever he enters my presence," she declared. " My blood not only tingles in my veins, but I sit as if benumbed or paralyzed."

" We must take good care then that he doesn't get into your presence again," returned Andree, with a seriousness not far removed from anxiety. "Without knowing a great deal about that man, we may safely assume that he is possessed of tremendous powers for evil."

" Oh, you should have seen his wicked eyes yesterday," exclaimed the girl, an irrepressible tremor passing over her. " His glance is like the thrust of a dagger."

" You must conjure up all your powers of resistance," suggested Mr. Haddon, " and also remain constantly on your guard against his further intrusions."

" I shall do so, of course, papa ; but I realize how powerless I am to avoid him or battle with him," returned Alice sadly. "What could any or all of us do, for instance, if he should choose to run his airship through The Eagle, thus hurling us to sure and swift destruction."

"True," assented Mr. Haddon, "but let us hope that we have given him the slip and that we may get out of harm's way before he can find us."

## CHAPTER VII.

*Getting Acquainted and Getting on Finely—A Sus-*
*picious Airship on the Horizon.*

IT was easier, however, to propose to be hopeful
than to realize anything like a feeling of security.
The thoughts of the explorers kept coming back to
Garvel, and the more they reflected upon the subjects suggested or revealed by the presence of this
mysterious stranger, the more completely were they
puzzled, interested and excited.

"You saw that he had no overcoat," resumed
Fraenckel, "and that is a suggestion that he doesn't
come from a cold country."

" The one great fact that his visit proclaims to
us," declared Dr. Strindberg, "is that there are people in the polar regions."

" Yes, a most singular people," agreed Mr. Haddon.

" Who navigate the air as easily as other people
navigate rivers and oceans," said Fraenckel.

"And since these people really exist," remarked Alice, "and have such extraordinary means of locomotion, why haven't they visited the great centres of civilization, New York, London and Paris?"

"It may be death for them to leave their country," suggested the clergyman.

"How death, papa?"

"Why, to begin with, they may not be able to live in any other climate than their own. Then, too, their government may have decreed that any citizen seeking to emigrate shall be executed."

"Another thing," said Andree, "these people may be patriotic enough to remain at home in order to prevent the great powers of the world from having any knowledge of their existence. They may have realized, as a people, that for them to be known is equivalent to being destroyed, as was the case with the natives of Spanish America, and even with the redskins."

"Be all that as it may," declared Fraenckel, "these natives are far ahead of us in certain points and features, as we have seen."

"Such as navigating the air," ventured the doctor. " But why didn't we ask Garvel to give us a lift northward ?"

" Particularly as he took it upon himself to speak of The Eagle as a 'tub,' " said Strindberg.

" Oh, I thought of asking him," avowed Andree.

" Then why didn't you ?" pursued the doctor.

" Simply because I foresaw he wouldn't do anything of the kind," affirmed the explorer. " He is so radically opposed to the object of our voyage that he would sooner see us die a thousand deaths than assist us to make a success of it."

" Is this your view of him ?" demanded the clergyman.

" I am almost ready to affirm that I know such are his sentiments."

" But why should he feel that way toward us ?" asked Alice.

" Such a feeling would be little more marked than the repugnance the Chinese have long manifested toward the ' outside barbarians '," said the explorer. " But these natives of the Polar Basin may have far better motives for their aversion to us than we can guess or imagine. For instance, suppose they live

on fruits and vegetables, or even take their nourishment in some more subtle and refined form, wouldn't
they have perfectly natural reasons, after looking
into our slaughter-houses, for regarding us as a race
of monsters ?"

"Well, I dare affirm that we are as good as that
Pirr Garvel," said Fraenckel.

"And it may be that they have excellent reasons
for wishing us to keep away from the Pole," suggested Alice. "For instance, it may be wholly
impossible for us to live in that latitude, if there is
as much electricity there as you seem to suppose,
Mr. Andree. Pirr Garvel confessed to me in so
many words that he would have died, if he had continued his journey a hundred miles south of the
point where we first encountered him."

"Indeed ! What reason did he give ?" asked the
explorer.

"Why, he said that the air was not strong enough
for him."

"Or that it was deficient in some of the elements
he required and too abounding in other qualities of
an obnoxious nature," said Mr. Haddon.  "What

he meant was that the air he found so far south was greatly unlike that he had been in the habit of breathing."   .

"Then may it not be that we shall labor under a similar disadvantage when we get over the rim of the Arctic Circle ?" asked Alice.

"Hardly," answered Andree. "The fact is, many of us have been well into the eighties without experiencing any particular trouble with the cold or with the air we were breathing. But enough of all this for the present," he added, with a shiver. "It is time for us to be looking out for a little warmth and nutriment in the shape of a pot of coffee."

"Hadn't we better take in those fragments of the guide-ropes ?" asked the doctor.

"For what reason ?" returned Andree. "There's little danger of any further entanglements, as we are at least fifteen hundred feet above the earth's surface."

"I know that," declared Strindberg, earnestly, "but that Garvel is our enemy—our deadly enemy —who has doubtless been sent out to make away with us, in case we don't perish through our own schemes, and I'm afraid he may steam under us and hook on to those ropes, towing us away to some retreat where his will may be supreme, and where we'd have a mighty poor show for ever reaching the North Pole or seeing old Sweden."

The manner of Andree showed that he was greatly impressed by these represeentations.

" There's a great deal of truth under what you are saying," he responded. " The infatuation of Pirr Garvel for Miss Alice may be a saving clause for us, however, so long as she is with us. We'll take in the ropes." And it was done accordingly.

"Another thing," then remarked Fraenckel, " at least two of us had better keep watch and ward to-night, one on each side of the basket, so that that airship cannot approach us without our knowing it."

" All right, we'll see about that later," responded Andree. " The business just now in hand is to get warm and have supper."

The sun was now swooping down to its lowest declension, disappearing behind a bank of clouds, which covered the whole western horizon, and the

dull, gray shadows of the afternoon were beginning
to take deeper hues.

And what a wild waste of water, snow and
ice was that upon which the canopy of sky and
gathering shadows rested! What stillness, too, was
that reigning everywhere—above, below and
around! The voiceless, unbroken quiet of Nature's
vastest solitudes, where man is a feeble intruder,
and where death reigns supreme from age to age
in an awful silence!

The scene impressed Andree to such an extent,
as he set about making his pot of coffee under the
helpful and interested glances of Alice, that he could
not help quoting the immortal lines of Poe :

> " By a route obscure and lonely,
> Haunted by ill angels only,
> Where an Eidolon named Night,
> On a black throne reigns upright,
> I have wandered home but newly
> From this ultimate dim Thule !"

"I suppose we may regard Pirr Garvel as the
'ill angel' of our route?" queried Alice, almost
gayly, so great was her delight at having Andree
between her and her persecutor.

"Yes, we may," returned the young explorer, his glances coming back to her with all the bold ardor of an honest affection.

"As to whether we ever 'wander home' from this 'ultimate dim Thule,'" said the clergyman, "that is a problem we may leave in the hands of an Infinite Father. If not to a home in this world, we may safely and surely reach that one which has been provided for us in the world to come."

Imagine a great basket divided into several compartments for food and other stores, including clothes, medicines and oil for cooking and lighting——

But all these preparations and arrangements for the voyage have been so often described in the newspapers of the world that we need make here only a passing allusion to them.

A corner was found for Alice where she could have the privacy and repose so essential to her, and her father was also provided with such a resting-place near her as he needed, the three hardy Swedes declaring that he should not be called

upon for the least care and fatigue in the handling
of The Eagle.

"The air is getting crisp and biting," reported
Andree after supper, proceeding to take a farewell
look into the gathering gloom with the aid of his
field-glass, "and we must prepare for it. We'll
make everything as snug as we can, and try to get
rested against the inevitable dangers and difficulties of to-morrow."

"How are we getting on?" asked Mr. Haddon,

"Finely," was the answer. "The breeze is beginning to develop its strength and is already bearing us onward some fifteen miles an hour."

"We can say good-by to Pirr Garvel, then," exclaimed Alice jubilantly—"good-by forever!"

"I don't know about that," returned Andree, his brow suddenly clouding, as he lowered his glass. "I see an ominous speck on our northwestern horizon. I believe Pirr Garvel is coming! An aerial craft is certainly afloat yonder, and who else than Pirr Garvel can be in it?"

## CHAPTER VIII.

*The Torpedo Balloon—Another Mysterious Naviga-
tor of the Air.*

A STICK thrust into a nest of hornets could not
have produced a quicker commotion than did the
announcement of Andree respecting the moving
object in the air he had noticed upon the horizon.

"Where is he?" asked Strindberg. "Let me
see him."

He raised the glass his leader had been using,
and sent a long glance through it in the direction
of the object claiming their attention.

"What is it?" demanded Fraenckel, becoming
impatient with his associate's lengthy scrutiny and
silence.

"Merely a speck as yet," replied the doctor.

"Is it coming this way?"

"It's too soon to decide.  Take a look at it."

Fraenckel hastened to gratify his curiosity, and
in due course Mr. Haddon and Alice did likewise,

"Well, what do you all make it out to be?" demanded Andree, looking around upon his fellow-travellers.

"I can only tell you what it isn't," responded the doctor. "It isn't the airship we saw two days ago, just as we were leaving Dane's Island out of sight behind us."

"Most assuredly an airship of some kind," ventured Fraenckel.

"But not the one in which Pirr Garvel has been in the habit of coming off to the wreck," declared Mr. Haddon.

"No, not that one," confirmed Alice. "To begin with, it's too low and too narrow, as well as totally unlike the Garvel craft. I see nothing whatever of those two large aluminum screws by which the Garvel ship—as he himself explained to us—is raised into the air and kept afloat in it."

"It looks like a huge torpedo," announced Andree, who, glass in hand, had resumed the study of the disquieting intruder. "All I can say at present is that it is coming this way, not exactly to ward us, but in such a way as to cross the route along which we are drifting."

" What !    With the. intention of intercepting us ?" queried Fraenckel.

" No doubt of it !"

" Then the thing can be steered ?"

" As directly as a train follows its track ! Look at it again."

The doctor hastened to comply.

" Sure enough," he commented, at the end of a few moments of earnest scrutiny.  " It's a balloon above all things, or, at least, an airship, but it is a motor in the shape of a large torpedo."

" Is it possible ?" queried Mr. Haddon.

" Please see for yourself, sir."

The clergyman bent another long glance through the instrument, and Alice could not help noticing that a tremor of intense surprise, not to say dread, passed over him.

" There can be no doubt about it," he reported. " It's a balloon in the shape of an immense torpedo, and moving in a straight line, precisely as a torpedo advances when shot from a ship !"

" But what keeps it afloat ?"

" Impossible to say."

The field-glass was now passed from hand to hand in rapid succession, and a general consensus of opinion in regard to the strange visitant was speedily forthcoming.

It was a torpedo balloon, advancing swiftly, driven by steam.

One seeing it suddenly might have easily mistaken it for a premonitory symptom of delirium, or for a complete hallucination of the senses.

" Is it moving faster than we are, papa ?" asked Alice.

" Yes ; two miles to our one !"

The whole situation was so singular that hardly another word was exchanged by the explorers and their guests until the extraordinary craft was less than a mile distant.

" I see a man in it," then annnounced Andree, who was again handling the glass, " only one.  He occupies a little perch, hardly larger than a chair, amidships, if I may use the word."

"So as to have a good view of his route," suggested Fraenckel.

"There may be another man or two in the body of the torpedo, as engineer or fireman," remarked the doctor. "Such is doubtless the case."

"Garvel was attended by two men in those capacities, as he himself told us!" said the clergyman, "and it's not easy to comprehend how any craft of this kind can be handled without such assistance."

The strange visitant now filled every eye to such an extent as to silence any and every attempt to give expression to the impressions of the observers. The man Andree had noticed was seen to be steering the craft by means of a sort of keyboard upon a raised shelf in front of him, and it was a marvel to see how quickly the course of the airship responded to his slightest pressure upon those keys.

"He certainly intends to speak us!" exclaimed Fraenckel, when the aerial torpedo had arrived within a quarter of a mile of The Eagle.

"Or to run us down!" supplemented Andree, a

little nervously. " Please hand me out my rifle, doctor."

The latter hastened to do so, and this hint of self-defense was not only observed by the unknown, but it brought a smile to his features.

He was a man very much in the style of Pirr Garvel, as regards build, complexion and aspect, but appeared to be of a milder and more humane type, his glances and features not possessing those lawless, wild and violent traits which had caused the good clergyman to term his menacing intruder the Polar Devil.

" Now, why was not that sort of machine thought of before ?" Fraenckel could not help exclaiming, so completely was he carried away by the ease with which the torpedo balloon kept afloat and advanced. " It swims in the air just as easily as a fish swims in the water !"

" Yes, it's wonderful," returned the doctor, " This machine is even a greater miracle than Garvel's."

Continuing to advance steadily until within hailing distance of the explorers, the extraordinary craft slackened speed until its progress corresponded to that of The Eagle, and it was then placed alongside, keeping within fifty yards of the balloon.

"I hope you are well, Mr. Andree," greeted the stranger, lifting his hat and bowing.

"I never felt better, sir, thank you," returned the explorer, accepting the greeting, and the excellent English in which it was spoken, as a matter of course. "And how are you, sir?"

"In fine shape, as usual. I thought I recognized the balloon as the one which had been filling at Dane's Island. When did you start northward?"

Andree told him.

"And contrary winds have brought you here?"

"That's just the situation, sir."

"Well, haven't you had about enough of this sort of thing?"

"How enough of it?"

"Are you not getting discouraged?"

"Not a bit of it," answered Andree. "We are moving on finely."

"For the moment—yes. But this breeze is no good for you. It will die out before morning.'

"That remains to be seen."

"Your balloon will explode, if, by any chance you should get over into the Polar Basin."

"Why should it ?"

"Because the electrical and other conditions there are so different."

"You speak as one who knows," said the Swede, smilingly. "Is there any other peril menacing us ?"

"Yes, many more than you would be willing to believe—perils of the most deadly description ! Let me give you a word of friendly advice, and that is to give up your proposed trip northward."

"I'm much obliged to you, I'm sure, for this unexpected interest in me," returned the explorer, his smile deepening, "but I cannot turn back. May I ask who you are, sir ?"

"My identity is of no consequence in this connection," returned the unknown, "but my name is Swib Neerec."

"Where do you live, Mr. Neerec ?"

"That also is foreign to the risks you are running," said the visitor, with a deprecating smile. "Didn't you have any difculty in getting clear of Dane's Island?"

"Our guide-ropes got entangled in some way, if that is what you mean," replied Andree.

"Tell me just what happened, please."

The explorer did so.

"And didn't you see anything of Pirr Garvel about that time?"

"To be sure."

"Please tell me under what circumstances."

## CHAPTER IX.

*The Mysteries of the Unknown Northland Increas-
ing and Deepening—Pirr Garvel again !*

IT suddenly occurred to the explorer that he
might be giving more information than he was getting.

" Is Garvel your friend ?" he demanded, after a
few moments of rapid reflection.

" Not exactly a friend—merely a colleague, a
fellow-official."

" I saw you were two of a kind," avowed Andree,
" if only by the oddness of your names. Do you
know where he is?"

" No, sir," confessed Neerec. " To be candid,
his movements have been very erratic for a week
or two, as if—— But when and where have you
seen him ?"

" The day we left Dane's Island, or day before
yesterday," responded Andree. " I've no objec-

tion to giving you the scanty particulars of our
meeting."

He proceeded to do so.

"And is that all that passed between you?"
asked Neerec.

"Substantially. But my friends here"—he indicated Mr. Haddon and Alice, who had raised
themselves into view—"have seen a good deal
more of him than I have and can tell you more
about him."

"If you will be so kind," said the visitor, saluting the father and daughter, and then permitting
his gaze to rest in a long glance of admiration
upon the latter.

Mr. Haddon related accordingly how often Pirr
Garvel had intruded upon him and Alice at the
wreck, and to what end, and this communication
seemed to interest Mr. Neerec immensely.

"Ah, this accounts for his dodging me lately,
and for his erratic movements, his disinclination for
my company and his eternal absences," commented
the visitor. "I thought something unusual had

come over him.   When and where did you see him last, Miss Haddon ?"

" No longer ago than yesterday," was the girl's answer.

" Where were you at that time ?   In about what latitude and longitude ?"

The clergyman told him.

" You have no idea where he is now ?"

" No, sir."

" But he seems to be thoroughly infatuated with your daughter, does he ?"

" That's only too evident."

" So much infatuated, in fact, that he will endeavor to see her again ?"

The clergyman nodded.

" Even though he knows she regards him with utter aversion ?"

" Such is the case, sir."

" You will be likely to have another visit from him, if he can find you ?"

" Undoubtedly."

" Then I had better keep an eye upon you, per-haps, as the surest way of finding him ?"

"Assuredly," answered the clergyman. "Are you very anxious to know where he is?"

"Very," confessed Neerec. "I knew he was under the spell of some new influence, but I little suspected its real nature."

Turning to Andree he resumed:

"And has this man done you no harm thus far?"

"Not the least, as far as we know," answered the explorer. "Possibly—but I will not accuse him."

"Well, that is singular."

The stranger seemed to lose himself in thought.

"If you think we are badly equipped for our proposed voyage," suggested Andree, after a pause, "why not take us aboard of your craft and give us free passage to Latitude Ninety?"

"Oh, I couldn't do that," returned Neerec. "You are jesting, surely. No one can live in Latitude Ninety—especially no one of your build and material."

"Again you speak as if posted!" commented Andree. "But let me insist upon your taking us with you if you are really anxious about us,"

The stranger shook his head.

" I couldn't do it," he repeated.

" Then what are you here for, anyhow ?" asked
Andree testily.

" Well, I saw your balloon and was bound to
know who was in it, as I supposed the Andree
craft had failed to leave Dane's Island. You
won't take my advice, then, and give over this
foolhardy undertaking ?"

" Not just at present, thank you."

" Then let me give you a word of advice," said
the unknown.   " Beware of Pirr Garvel !"

" We intend to."

" Don't let him come near you or he'll destroy
you utterly—run you down, or fire a shot into you
that will blow you up !   He's after you !"

" Some miles after us, I hope," returned Andree,
smiling again.

" Well, I've at least done my duty by you," said
the stranger.   " Good-day, sir."

The explorer responded with a wave of the
hand, as the stranger put the torpedo balloon in
rapid motion and within five minutes thereafter the

second airship was disappearing from view upon the eastern horizon.

"Well, what next?" was the comment of Andree.

"In any case, it's evident we are far better known to these people than they are to us," remarked the doctor. "Is it too much to say that our proposed journey into the Polar Basin has been heralded in that quarter?"

"That's just what has happened!" declared Fraenckel. "The 'natives' have heard that we are coming, and they don't want us to come!"

"What's more, they are watching us!" declared Andree. "Both of these men—Garvel and Neerec—are patrolling these latitudes to keep us out!"

"Or head us off," suggested Mr. Haddon.

"Or get rid of us by some well-designed 'accident,'" declared Alice. "And isn't it quite possible, if we once make our way into the country of these people, that we shall never be allowed to leave it?"

Silence fell upon the whole group at this suggestion. Certainly, they were in a very singular situation.

But scarcely a minute had passed when Andree started violently, uttering a cry of astonishment.

"Heavens! Look there!" he cried, with outstretched hand. "Yonder he comes—the very man we are so anxious to avoid!"

There was no mistake about it this time. The screw balloon was already close at hand, looming out of the twilight and bearing down upon them!

## CHAPTER X.

### The Daring Enemy and How He Carried His Point.

THE identity of the approaching airship and that of its terrible occupant having been duly established, the explorer turned to Alice Haddon and her father.

" Down in the basket—out of sight !" he enjoined hurriedly. " It may be that Garvel doesn't know you are here and that he is not in pursuit of you."

" Oh, yes—yes ! I know that he is coming to claim me !" breathed the girl wildly.

" But we'll none the less get out of sight," said Mr. Haddon.

The couple stowed themselves away accordingly, silently praying that the dreadful peril by which they were menaced might be averted.

On came the pursuer, for such he was now seen to be, and ere long he was so near—that terrible man of the air—that they could see the gleaming of his eyes and hear his horrible chuckle of triumph as he shouted :

" Ha ! ha !  Is it thus we meet, fair Alice ?  Is it thus we meet, Herr Andree ?"

" Sheer off there !" thundered the explorer, who had seized his rifle and was handling it in such a way as to show that he would pick off the intruder if he came too near.  " Go your way, Pirr Garvel, and don't venture within range !"

A mocking laugh came from the pursuer at this adjuration.

" The air is free to everybody, as the old proverb will have told you, Herr Andree," he retorted scornfully, continuing to steer his craft in such a way as to place himself nearer and nearer ; " and I fancy I have as much right here as you, not to speak of the important business claiming my attention."

" Sheer off, I say !"

" Oh, don't get excited," sneered the mysterious suitor for the hand of Alice Haddon, as his craft took up a position within fifty yards of the balloon

and proceeded to make its speed and course con-
form to those of the explorers. " Don't be foolish,
Herr Andree.    I want no quarrel with you, but I
must have possession of that girl on the instant !"

"What girl ?" responded the explorer desper-
ately.

"Come !   Come !" retorted Pirr Garvel, with grim
scorn and mockery.   " Don't be like the ostrich,
Herr Andree, which hides its head in the sand and
imagines no one can see it !   Don't flatter yourself
that I didn't see you take Miss Haddon and her
father from the wreck, just because you didn't see
me !"

He flourished a field-glass which had nothing to
distinguish it externally from the one the explorer
had been so recently using, and added :

" Just note, sir, that I have here an instrument
whose powers are limited only by the convexity of
the earth's surface !   Didn't see you, eh ?   Didn't
see Miss Alice ascend the rope-ladder and so reach
the old tub in which you are on your way—whither?
Let me tell you that I even saw that sea-serpent
laying hold of that sperm whale for his dinner.''

A groan escaped Mr. Haddon, and found some sort of an echo from the lips of Andree and Alice.

"Oh, he saw us!" murmured the latter. "He knows we are here. It's useless to deny our presence or even conceal it."

"You see, therefore," resumed the pursuer, "that I am not making war upon you under idle or futile claims, but that I am here to recover the girl you have stolen from me. I want no quarrel with you, as I said, but——"

"Just keep your distance, will you?" called the explorer, who was again handling his rifle nervously.

"Come! Come!" enjoined Pirr Garvel again. "Do you mean to say that you are in a position to offer resistance? Just let me show you how easily I can sail under you and over you, around and beside you, high and low, here and there, just as if you were at rest on the earth's surface! Ha! Ha! Before you begin to make yourself disagreeable you should realize what an immense difference there is between your resources and mine!"

He had signalled his engineer while speaking,

and very strange and menacing were the evolutions
upon which he now entered, sailing around the balloon and over and under it, and clearly indicating
that he could destroy it at any moment by merely
touching one of the steering keys under his hand.

So evident was his mastery of the situation, so
useless all further attempts at concealment, that
the father and daughter did not hesitate to show
themselves, and they even watched these sinister
evolutions of their persecutor's air-ship with a
breathless fascination they could neither resist nor
conceal.

"There! You see what a bad time you will have, Herr Andree, if you should force me to be uncivil," said the pursuer, as he again placed his craft alongside the balloon. "Let me add merely that I have come here for that girl and that I shall have her. Will you give her up peacefully?"

"Never!"

"Then excuse the smoke."

Even as he ceased speaking, a jet of something resembling smoke left the nozzle he had raised into view and shot like a flash across the space between the airship and the balloon, striking full in their faces all the occupants of the latter.

"There! How's that for a beginning?" cried Pirr Garvel, his features aglow with scorn and triumph. "Is another dose necessary?"

Not a sound came from the balloon by way of response. The explorers and their guests had all dropped into so many heaps as if withered by lightning.

"It's all right, Vegg," exclaimed Garvel, addressing his engineer, who had appeared in the narrow staircase leading from the hull of the airship to the steering-box. " They've gone to sleep. Take my place here and lay the nose of The Flyer against the basket of the balloon."

This measure was executed promptly, and Pirr Garvel climbed to the top of the balloon basket, surveying with a grim smile of triumph the motion-less figures there presented.

" So much, my friends, for going to war without the necessary resources," he muttered. " With age and experience the Swede may do better."

Gathering Alice to his breast with as much ap-parent ease as if she had been a child, he retraced his steps to his own craft, and in another moment was leaving the balloon behind him with a rapidity resembling the eagle's flight.

# CHAPTER XI.

## *Pirr Garvel and Alice.*

A SINGLE glance was enough to tell Alice, when she opened her eyes, that she had been transferred from the basket of the balloon to the hull or cabin of the airship. And yet this change of place was so surprising—especially the method of it—that she found it difficult to credit the evidence of her senses.

" Can it be ?" she murmured.

Making an effort to rise she found herself powerless to do so, as if paralyzed.

" You ought to know where you are, dearest," said Pirr Garvel, thus calling her attention to the fact that he sat beside her.

" Ah ! I'm in your airship !"

"Yes ; in the cabin of The Flyer."

The captive recognized the fact not merely because of the cigar-shaped outlines of the cabin, but also because Pirr Garvel had shown her and Mr. Haddon through it on the occasion of one of his early visits to the wreck.

" How long have I been here ?" she demanded.

Her abductor looked at his watch.

" Just forty minutes," he answered.

"And how "—

The words died away in an incoherent murmur, she was suddenly seized by such an awful terror.

"How did you come here?" he said. "The question is only too natural. I brought you here from the basket of the balloon in which you were running away from me."

" Ah, I remember. A strange smoke shot out from the airship and struck us !" cried Alice. "We fell as if dead. I remember the horrible sensation of falling. Did you hurt papa?"

"Certainly not—the parent of my own darling, with whom I expect to pass the rest of my days in rapture ! I should say not. What a question."

" Did you harm Mr. Andree ?"

" Not in the least, dear."

" Will they recover their senses as I have ?"

"Certainly; as you have."

" What was that stuff with which you sprinkled us?"

"Oh, I'm not obliged to answer such questions as that until you become my regular partner in business."

" And where is the balloon now?"

" Drifting on in the same direction we are taking—but don't scream, dear. It's so far away already that your friends cannot possibly hear you."

The girl had arisen, with parted lips, but at this injunction she sank back upon the cushioned seat she had found herself occupying at the moment of her return to consciousness.

" I see a dismal fog has set in!" she ejaculated. " What awful darkness! Do you mean to say that you can keep trace of that balloon in such gloom as this?"

" I can and I shall!"

" How is that possible?"

" That's another of my secrets!"

" Tell me! I implore you!"

" Nothing is easier.　The balloon has been show-ing lights ever since night set in."

" Impossible !" cried Alice.　" It was agreed and well understood by all of us that no gleam of light should betray our whereabouts to you !"

" Nevertheless, we are duly enlightened."

He beckoned her to one of the windows of the cigar-shaped hull.

" See there !" he added.　"Yonder.　Let me raise the window," and he suited his action to the word.　" Yonder, a mere gun-shot distant.　Don't you see a faint row of lights—some half dozen or more ?"

" Yes, I see them."

" Good.　Those lights are on The Eagle, and you will realize how easy it is for me to find her at any hour of the night."

" But how came those lights there ?"

" To begin with, they are not really lights, as we understand that word."

" What then ?"

" Merely phosphorescent gleams, to speak in terms suited to your comprehension," explained

Garvel. " I painted them there before the balloon left Dane's Island."

" And they show only in the dark ?"

" Only in the dark, and when there is considerable darkness. In fact, the greater the darkness the more plainly are they visible."

"And Mr. Andree knows nothing of them ?"

" Not the least thing ! They are arranged in a row above the middle of the balloon, so that they cannot possibly be seen from the basket below. It is as easy, therefore, for me to keep track of The Eagle as it would be for you to cross one of the streets of New York by the aid of an electric light."

Alice stared at him in a terror of amazement.

" Did you know beforehand that Mr. Andree was intending to start upon this voyage ?"

" Yes, for months."

He reflected deeply, and added :

" To be frank with you, I came very near demolishing his balloon before he was ready for departure."

" You did ?  Why ?"

"Because I foresaw days and days in advance that he would be carried to the wreck—as he actually was carried thither—and that he was almost certain to come between you and me!"

"Ah! You foresaw this?"

"As clearly as I see you at this moment," he affirmed with a sincerity she could not doubt, waving her back to her seat and resuming his own in front of her. "I will even confess," he added, sinking his voice to a whisper, so that it would not reach the hearing of his man at the head of the companion-way, "that I made an effort to bring the expedition to naught at the very moment Andree entered upon it."

"Tell me how, please."

He proceeded to describe how he had fouled the guide-ropes by dissembling the trailing ends of them under some rocks and beams near the balloon-house on Dane's Island, and finished with a hollow and contented laugh, saying:

"You should have seen the start! I wonder even now how the balloon and its occupants failed to be dashed to pieces!"

"Mr. Andree had you for an enemy then, even before his departure?"

"Yes, because I feared he would encounter you and become my rival!"

"That was a long look ahead and a very difficult one, I should think," commented Alice.

"Not for any one as well posted as I am in regard to all the breezes and air currents of this region. But how do you like Mr. Andree?"

The sudden question brought to the girl's face one of those beautiful blushes which only a loving heart can paint, and the arch-schemer was answered.

"I see!" he muttered, a fiendish scowl corrugating his features. "This meddling Swede is already as dear to you as I am obnoxious!"

"I will not deny it!" cried Alice, calling to her aid her courage and energy. "And let this fact tell you now and here, Mr. Garvel, how vain and useless are all the persecutions and vexations of which I am the object. I shall never, never give you the least thought of love—not even ordinary

respect.   You may as well restore me to my friends
now as later.   Oh, will you ?"

She sprang to her feet, with clasped hands, and
stood before him in an attitude of the wildest be-
seeching.

"Yes, I'll return you to them—when the whole
Arctic Ocean has become boiling hot ; but not before, I swear it !''

He made a savage gesture, before which she recoiled to her seat, and there she sat staring at him,
shivering and benumbed, as if her every faculty
were bound in icy fetters.

"You—you didn't kill papa ?" she finally man-
aged to articulate.

"Haven't I told you I didn't do him the least
harm ?"

"Nor Mr. Andree ?"

"No, I didn't harm him."

"And how long will it be before they recover
their senses ?"

"Oh, not long—perhaps half an hour or three-
quarters."

"Then, how is it that I recovered so quickly ?"

" Oh, I gave you the necessary remedy, a snuff of these salts," explained her captor, holding up to her view a small vial.   " The truth is, I didn't want to wait the ordinary course of things.   Your society is too precious to me not to have hastened your recovery."

"Whither are we bound?"

" I don't know as I ought to tell you," he responded.  " Perhaps I have not yet decided what to do with you.  It is enough to say that any destination I reach with you will be the right one."

" And what do you expect to gain by this violence ?"

" I expect to teach your father and you that I am master of the situation.  Both of you are in my power, and at my mercy.  From this moment onward you are mine beyond redemption."

He saw that she was hardly able to retain possession of her senses, so terribly was she prostrated by her situation.

" I will leave you now," he added, waving his hand to a snug little stateroom at one end of the craft, " but would advise you to try to sleep, as there'll be a lively time at our house to-morrow !"

A groan escaped Alice as he sauntered on deck. How horrible was her situation !

## CHAPTER XII.

*In the Polar Basin—The Forest of Mastodons—
A House !*

IT was with an awful sinking of the heart that
Andree came back to consciousness from his sudden
and unnatural sleep into which he and his friends
had been thrown by the noxious vapor showered
upon them by Garvel.

"I remember !" he ejaculated, gaining his feet.
"Are you awake, Mr. Haddon ?"

"Yes; just arousing from the horrible sleep in-
duced by that man's poisons ! And Alice ?"

"I—I have not heard her speak yet," faltered
the explorer, an awful anxiety oppressing him.
"Perhaps she hasn't recovered."

"I am all right," said Fraenckel, gathering himself up into a sitting posture.

"And I," affirmed the doctor.  "The rascal evidently did not mean to kill us."

"No," returned Andree, "for he could just as well have done that as to do what he did."

"Alice, my child," faltered Mr. Haddon, gathering himself up slowly from the bottom of the basket, "have you recovered your senses?"

There was no answer.

"Speak, my dear Alice.'

Still the same silence.

"For heaven's sake, my dear friend, let's have a light," demanded the clergyman, in a voice that was husky and almost inaudible with the expectancy of a great horror.

The light was duly produced and the anxious father hastened to investigate. One glance around was enough. The place Alice had occupied was empty!

"Gone!" exclaimed the father, hardly able to articulate.

"That terrible wolf of the air has been here, of course," cried Andree. "He has been here while we all lay as silent and motionless as dead men, and has carried her off!"

It required no great prescience on the part of the

four men to conjure up the scene of the abduction substantially as it had taken place.

"Well, it's something that he did not kindle a fire in our midst or otherwise destroy us," commented Strindberg. "He has spared us for some reason."

"Perhaps he has let me live with a view to utilizing me later in his persecution of my poor child," sighed Mr. Haddon. "She is in his hands, certain."

"It would be useless—nay, hurtful—to shut our eyes to the fact," affirmed Andree, with forced calmness. "That villain has seized Miss Alice, and is carrying her whither he will, while we are drifting along here in utter helplessness, unable even to take care of ourselves."

He finished with a groan of anguish, in such a state of anguish and excitement that he had to cling to the rim of the basket for support.

"Well, there is one gleam of hope for us," the doctor hastened to say, not merely for his own consolation, but for the encouragement of his associates and Mr. Haddon. "That Swib Neerec hinted that he would keep an eye on us, and it may be that he will trace Pirr Garvel to his lair and restore the poor girl to us."

"That is, indeed, within the bounds of possibility," said Mr. Haddon, catching at the straw thus offered him. "In the meantime, what can we do, Mr. Andree? Make an attempt to follow the monster?"

"As if we could! I can only repeat what I've said before—namely, that we can only go whither we are drifted and driven."

"While that atrocious miscreant can cleave the air like a bird, going where he will," groaned Mr. Haddon. "Oh, we ought to have remembered that he has the powers of a demon, and to have remained on our guard against him."

"It's not easy to see what we could have done," said the doctor, trying to call to his aid all the calmness and philosophy he was in the habit of preaching.

"The villain would have run his airship through our balloon if we had offered any resistance."

Making all snug again, Andree resumed a crouching posture on the floor of the balloon basket.

"I will not despair," he proclaimed, with his wonted energy, "nor will you, Mr. Haddon. Let us call what hope and patience we can to our aid, and wait for new developments."

He produced from his medical stores a powerful opiate, handing to his companions a liberal dose of it, and helping himself, with the best of results, for all of them were soon asleep, and it was only after hours of unbroken repose, that they awoke to the light of another morning.

Andree was the first one astir, and it was his exclamations of joy and surprise that aroused his companions.

"Can any of you guess how far we have come?" he demanded.

"Of course not," answered Fraenckel, with a view to securing his good news as soon as possible.

"Well, we've come about eight hours at something like thirty miles an hour," explained Andree, "and now just figure for yourselves. We have come about two hundred and forty miles due north since last evening, and are less than this number of miles from the Pole."

"In other terms, we are where no other person from Europe or America has ever been," declared Dr. Strindberg, his eyes kindling as they had never kindled before.

"And just imagine what there is beneath us," resumed Andree, his features aglow with an intense joy and satisfaction. "Or, rather, let me tell you, for you could never imagine—never! Green fields, to begin with, yet fields which are almost in touch with glaciers and snow-topped mountains, precisely as you see them in Switzerland and other parts of Europe, nothing more or less than we all expected."

He had gently detained his associates while speaking, but he now allowed them to look out upon the scene he had depicted, watching them with a radiant contentment.

"Ah, how glorious!" ejaculated Fraenckel, with the rapture only known to hopes and beliefs which have been realized. "Did I not always tell you so? Haven't we all known it?"

"At last! At last!" was the cry of Strindberg, who tossed his hands and arms as wildly as if seeking to embrace a celestial vision.  "What joy to find one's hopes so nobly fruitful!  To see as reality what we have so long seen as dreams!"

The ejaculations of the couple could not have failed to arouse Mr. Haddon, terribly as he was oppressed by the grief to which he had awakened. He gained his feet slowly, and turned his eyes upon the scene beneath him.

"It's true, then, Mr. Andree?" he cried, a flush of joy driving the pallor from his face.  "God has indeed been good to us.  We have reached a sure and vivid promise of the better things to come."

"As you see," explained the explorer, "we have passed the 'icy barrier' during our sleep and have reached the milder zone beyond it.  What a change in a few hours' travel.  Note the great forest on the right, with the river dividing it, and—yes! see those mastodons feeding on the edge of the open plains beyond!"

"Sure enough!" responded Mr. Haddon.  "It is a herd of those monsters which has come down to us in a direct line of descent from the prehistoric ages!  I remember reading in an American paper that a herd similar to this had been discovered and hunted in Alaska."

For a few moments the four men contemplated these descendants of the shaggy and formidable occupants of the primeval world as they fed, played and fought in all their native wildness.

" Oh, if my poor child were only with us ! If the scene before us could only be enjoyed with her," exclaimed the unhappy father.

" Courage, Mr. Haddon," enjoined the explorer. " We'll soon have her with us again.   I cannot, will not doubt it.   Is not the scene before us what you anticipated ?"

" It is—even to human occupancy !" literally shouted the clergyman, with an excitement he could not command.   " Look there !"

" Just where, please ?" asked the doctor, with a voice and manner which attested that everything swam around him, such was his excitement.

" There !" cried Mr. Haddon, with outstretched hand.   " There, on the bank of the river.   A house !  A human habitation !   Look, all of you !"

## CHAPTER XIII.

*Another Descent to Terra Firma—The Situation Getting Critical.*

THE scene their gaze encountered held the explorers speechless a number of minutes.

" Surely this is a goodly land," then said Mr. Haddon : " such a country, Mr. Andree, as you started out to find.   Shall we not descend to it— take footing upon it ?"

" We shall have to do so, or be blown back where we came from," responded the explorer. "Curious, is it not, that such a fine breeze should bring us across the 'Icy Barrier' into the great polar depression of which I was speaking, and then die out abruptly ?"

" Yes, it is certainly exceptional," returned the doctor, " but there's no doubt about it.   We are becalmed again, certain !"

It was impossible to ignore the fact, The Eagle

having become stationary almost directly over the house which had fixed the clergyman's attention.

"We must act at once—before the wind begins carrying us in the other direction," said Andree, after carefully noting the leading facts and pointers of the situation. "Are our ballast lines long enough?"

"Ample," replied Fraenckel. "I added six hundred feet after we drew in the guide-ropes last evening."

"Then let's act instantly," proposed the explorer, passing over the rim of the basket the anchor he had used on the occasion of his visit to the wreck. "Pay me out as rapidly as possible."

He planted himself upon the flukes of the anchor, as was his wont, and his associates hastened to lower him.

"I see nothing in the shape of human beings," resumed the explorer, "but that is no proof of their non-existence. Yet I have my idea of this region, which I may as well mention. We are in a sort of borderland between the 'Icy Barrier' and the country we are seeking."

"No doubt of it," came from Fraenckel, who, with the doctor, was paying out the ballast line as rapidly as was safe or easy.

"Ah! there's a puff from the north," was Andree's next observation. "See! It is taking us, very slowly, though, to that group of pines just to the north of the house. If we could pull the balloon down into that shelter and secure her before the wind rises, she would ride out quite a gale without losing much of her hydrogen."

"Oh, we shall do that," assured the doctor, with his accustomed clear-cut view of the situation. "As soon as you've landed and made fast we'll haul the balloon down and secure it."

At the end of a few minutes Andree reached the earth and secured the balloon by passing the ballast line and anchor around a lower limb of one of the pines of which he had spoken.

"Haul her down," he ordered.

The task seemed a long one, under the eagerness and excitement of the moment, but it was eventually accomplished, the balloon being hauled down as near to the ground as it could be, in such a position as to be sheltered, not to say hidden.

"There! Throw out your rope ladder and come down," was Andree's next order.

The trio hastened to comply. Mr. Haddon taking the lead, and the doctor bringing up the rear, with quite an arsenal of rifles and revolvers.

"We've lightened her a good deal, so many of us getting out," said the explorer, looking up at the balloon, as a puff of wind struck it, causing it to sway to one side and tug at the ballast line severely. "Just how well she is going to stand that sort of thing remains to be seen, but we'll keep an eye on her."

"Let's divide up these weapons," proposed Strindberg, proceeding to pass them around. "If we encounter a squad of Polar men or electrical men, or an enemy in human form of any kind, we shall present a good deal better front with them than without them."

Acting upon these suggestions, the four men took possession of their weapons, and proceeded to give close attention to their immediate surroundings.

"Ah ! see here !" exclaimed the clergyman, before he had gone a dozen yards.  "The airship of
Pirr Garvel !"

There could be no doubt upon this head, the
craft bearing in several places its name : The Flyer.

"He has arrived here ahead of us," continued
Mr. Haddon, a prey to the wildest excitement,
"and is it not possible that the house we have seen
is his habitation ?"

"Of course it is his, or one he is occupying, or
The Flyer would not be here," responded Strindberg.  "But his men—his engineer and fireman—
where are they ?"

"Asleep, of course, as they've had to be awake
all night to make the journey hither," suggested
Fraenckel.  "They are either at the house or on
the airship itself—most likely the latter. Let's
see."

He stole cautiously to the entrance of the cigar-
shaped hull of the airship and found that his theory
was the correct one, the two men in question being
extended at full length under blankets on the floor
of the cabin.

Announcing the fact by pressing his finger to his lips, Fraenckel stole back to his companion.

"Their employer is evidently here for more than a passing stay," he suggested. "At any rate, the fire is out under the boilers of The Flyer, and she could not be put afloat without due preparation."

"So far, so good," growled the doctor. "Ought we to seize and bind these men on the instant, thus putting it out of their power to make war upon us ?"

"What do you think, Mr. Haddon ?" demanded Andree.

"The measure is unnecessary, if these are all the men at Garvel's immediate disposal," replied the clergyman. "Let's leave them undisturbed for the moment and search for their employer. That he's in this house is more than suggested by the presence of the airship and its crew, and it's no less certain that my daughter is here with him. Let's take our way to the entrance ———"

"Silence ! Follow me !" interrupted Andree, with a start of the wildest excitement. "This way, all ! Let's get to cover. Yonder comes the torpedo balloon of Neerec !"

A single glance was enough to tell the observers

the truth of this state-
ment, and that they all
hastened to conceal
themselves in a shed
which was used for the
storage of various sup-

plies belonging to the airship.

"It's coming here," continued the explorer, after
another glance at the approaching craft, "and it

will be a wise thing for us to let him precede us in
our visit to Pirr Garvel."

"You mean that a clash between these two men
is not only probable and possible, but that it is
likely to result to our advantage?" queried the
clergyman.

"Exactly.  If they come to hostilities they will
be fighting our battles."

A few suggestions and precautions succeeded,
and then all remained quiet on the part of the explorers, while Swib Neerec landed from his airship and hastened swiftly in the direction of the
house supposed to shelter Pirr Garvel.

"And here's another singular turn of fate," said
Andree.  "Neerec has carried his point! By following us, as he spoke of doing, he has been guided
to the hiding-place of his enemy—for enemies they
are, as you can see by the pale, drawn features of
the man who has just passed us."

The snapping of a rope succeeded, calling all eyes
in the direction of the balloon, and a general cry
of dismay escaped the observers.

The wind had increased rapidly, coming in puffs,

while they were busy with the arrival of Neerec, and a final severe strain had snapped the ballast line at the edge of the basket, leaving The Eagle free to take a swift flight into the heavens.

"Ah, God of mercy!" groaned the clergyman, his wild glances following the rapidly vanishing balloon. "That settles it. We can neither go on nor go back. Heaven help us!"

"Hold!" enjoined Andree, recovering from the sort of stupor which had momentarily dazed him. "We'll exchange The Eagle for The Flyer—our ' old tub ' for the latest invention!"

"And now to the rescue of my child," proposed Mr. Haddon. "Forward, all together! Lively!"

.

## CHAPTER XIV.

*Pirr Garvel and Alice Haddon Again—A Timely
Arrival.*

THE house which had fixed the attention of the
explorers, as related, was of two stories, and some
thirty feet by fifty.

It was built of rough, gray granite, and looked
old enough, in its setting of vines, to have existed
for ages.

In the dining-room of this house two persons sat
at breakfast, Pirr Garvel and his captive, the latter
looking as bright and cheerful as the morning
itself.

The room was poorly furnished, but the china
was ample and costly, bearing the name of the
host's airship, and the meal, which had been served
up to the couple was of the most elaborate and
appetizing description.

" Did you sleep well in your little stateroom
aboard The Flyer?" asked Garvel as he proceeded

to pour her coffee and help her to a piece of broiled steak.

"Never better," she replied ; "and I wouldn't have been my father's daughter if I hadn't."

"What do you mean by that ?"

"I simply mean that God will take care of us in all situations—so papa says—and that we have no cause to worry."

This simple faith caused Pirr Garvel to stir uneasily in his chair, and he hastened to change the subject.

"As I was saying when we came into the house from The Flyer, an hour ago," he said, entering upon his repast heartily, "we have known a number of months that Mr. Andree had decided to embark in his balloon for these regions. But you are not eating."

"I was simply waiting for you to set the example."

"To be sure that you wouldn't be drugged or poisoned, eh ?"

"That's it !"

"Well, you see that I have commenced opera-
tions ?"

"Yes, and I will now do likewise."

She began her breakfast accordingly.

"You were saying," she resumed, "that the proposed advent of Mr. Andree in these regions had
been duly announced to you ?"

"And not only was I sent out to intercept him,
in case his advance should be successful," continued her host, "but so also were others. The
fact is, you see, his project was regarded as a very
serious menace for interests of the gravest import-
ance !"

Alice inclined her shapely head understandingly,
without ceasing to do justice to the tempting
dishes before her, taking care, however, to honor
only those her entertainer had tasted.

"The essential point of our instructions," resumed Garvel, "was not to let Andree get further
north than we are at this moment !"

"I see !" commented Alice, tersely.

"We were further instructed," pursued her
captor, "not to let Andree return to Europe—

never! never!—in case he should reach this latitude in safety.   And the final point of our instructions, of course," he added, with a grim smile, " was
to let the ' daring explorer ' kill himself by his own
devices, if conditions were favorable."

"Well, he hasn't killed himself yet," returned
Alice, spiritedly, " and the chances are that he may
not."

"Be that as it may," resumed Pirr Garvel, "his
life and that of his associates, as also yours and
your father's, now depend upon you, Miss Alice!"

"Upon me, sir?   Explain!"

"If you will marry me," announced her admirer,
"I will rescue all your friends, including Herr Andree, from their present perilous situation, and will
stand between you and all trouble from this hour
onward!"

"You are very kind to yourself," replied the
girl, sarcastically. "Will you stand between us
and Mr. Neerec, for instance?"

The effect of this name upon Pirr Garvel was
like that of a blow.

"Neerec?" he ejaculated. "What do you know about him?"

"Very little, I must confess; but enough to show that he is as distinctly our friend as you are!"

"Has he seen you?"

"I won't deny it," returned Alice, with a smile intended to be a provocation.

"And—and did he experience the same sort of admiration for you that I did?"

"I cannot say just what he experienced, Mr. Garvel," replied the girl, "for the reason that the conditions were not favorable—he being in his balloon and we in ours—for the complete expansion of his sentiments!"

"But he fell in love with you, of course," declared Garvel, moving uneasily. "How could he help doing so?"

Pirr Garvel arose and locked the doors leading into the room, then returning to his chair.

"Let me come to the point of this interview," he resumed, listening a few moments, with a keen look around. "Time is pressing. Your father is a clergyman, and as such is empowered to solemnize a marriage in any quarter of the globe. Promise to be my wife—to marry me this morning, or as soon as your father is restored to you ——"

The girl interrupted him by a gesture of impatience.

" I can neither marry you nor make any promise about marrying you," she declared, with a firmness that was all the more apparent because of her quiet voice and manner. " As I have already indicated, I have given my heart to 'the Swede,' as you call Mr. Andree, and no other than he shall ever be my husband."

" Don't say that, foolish girl," enjoined the desperate wooer, his face aflame and his eyes glassy and menacing. " Your father and the Swede cannot be far distant at this moment, considering the fine breeze with which they have been favored, and I swear to you that I will be the death of them if you do not immediately give me your promise "—

" Never, sir—never !"

At this moment came a knock on the door leading from the kitchen.

"Who's there?" called Garvel, stepping in that direction.

"Erba," was the answer.

"Ah, my sister," exclaimed Garvel by way of explanation to Alice, "don't be alarmed."

He unlocked the door and opened it.

"The balloon of Andree has arrived," reported the newcomer, who was a thin, pale girl of a dozen years. "It was becalmed directly over us, and the explorers have descended from it."

"Good! Glorious!" commented Garvel, as the girl turned away. "Those men are now at my mercy!"

Closing the door he returned to Alice, making two or three energetic passes as he neared her.

"Did you hear the news?" he asked. "Your Andree has come!"

"He—he has?" faltered the girl with a bewildered air.

"Why, yes," assured Garvel, repeating his passes. "Don't you know me? I am here—your own loving Andree! Come to me!"

"Oh, nonsense!" cried Alice contemptuously,

giving him a push that nearly sent him prostrate. "Enough of that kind of chatter! Let me out of this place on the instant!"

"Not a step!" he responded angrily, grasping her arm. "Since fair means——"

He was interrupted by a scream from his captive, and the next instant an outer door was burst open with a crash, a man appearing on the threshold.

This man was Swib Neerec!

## CHAPTER XV.

*The Two Rivals and Alice Haddon—A Glimpse of the Real State of Affairs at the North Pole.*

THE manner of Swib Neerec, as he thus burst into the presence of his "colleague" and Alice, was violent in the extreme, as if he were laboring under some irrepressible excitement.

And indeed he was.

The mere glimpse he had caught of the girl while she and her father were giving him, from their balloon basket, the details of the persecutions to which they had been subjected by Garvel, had inspired him with the one great and overwhelming passion of his life.

He did not merely love her—love her madly and selfishly on her own account and because of her rare loveliness, charms and grace, but he loved her all the more fiercely because of his relations to Garvel.

By just so much as he hated his associate, by just

so much was his sudden passion for Alice inflamed and magnified.

" So this is the secret of your conduct during the last fortnight," cried the intruder; " the secret of your absences and dodgings !"

' Ah, it is you, my boy." returned Garvel, without displaying the slightest disturbance of voice or manner. " Come in ! Miss Haddon and I have just finished our breakfast, but if you haven't had yours and don't mind eating alone—why pull up your chair——'

" Thanks, but I have breakfasted," interrupted Neerec, with icy scorn and reprobation.

" And are ready for business, eh ?" returned Garvel. " At your disposal, sir. For what are you here ?"

" To rescue this young lady from your vile persecutions."

" I don't think she wants to be rescued by you."

" Oh, yes, she does. I can ask her."

" No, I don't want you to waste your time on me, Mr. Neerec," said Alice, who had seen through a window her father and Andree descending from their balloon, and who accordingly knew that they were near her. " I have no wish to be rescued— none whatever."

" You hear, don't you, my dear Swib ?" sneered Pirr Garvel, expanding his chest and smiling. " The young lady doesn't want to be rescued; she doesn't want anything to do with you."

" That's because she doesn't know how danger- ous you are," retorted the new-comer. " But I'll expose you !"

" Proceed, one or ooth of you," enjoined Alice, dropping back into the chair from which she had arisen. " The one that talks fastest and the most to the point, that man shall have me for his friend!"

" That one shall be me," assured Neerec. " What is it that you wish to know ?"

" Everything—who you are, where you came from, what you are doing here, who feeds you, and so on for two or three octavo volumes. If you have a tongue, Mr. Neerec, now's your time to use it."

" I will," replied the new-comer, placing a chair

in front of her and planting himself in it.   Where shall I begin?"

"Begin with this man," and she indicated Gar-vel, who had hastily seized a chair and deposited himself beside his rival.   "Would you believe it, Mr. Neerec, this man has been hounding me for two weeks to marry him, and he hasn't told me a single word about himself, his birth and breeding —or want of it—his nationality, the state of his finances, or any of those details it is customary and necessary to furnish on such occasions!"

"That's just like him," declared the new-comer. "He's no good, anyhow.   He's the very last man in the world you want to own as even a speaking acquaintance.   But ask me what you will.   I'm ready to answer."

"Then who is this man?"

"He's a capta, or centurion—say, orderly ser-geant—in the service of the King of Polaria."

"And what are you?"

"I am a capta in that same service."

"And which of you is the ranking capta?"

"Neither of us; we are equals.   "I've no orders

to take from him and none to give him. Our juris-
dictions are detached and separate, and this is his,
mine being fifty miles to the northeastward. As
far as you are concerned, Miss Haddon, I propose
to be the ranking capta."

"Well, you won't be," growled Pirr Garvel savagely.

"Tell me now, Mr. Neerec," resumed Alice,
"what you mean by that term, the King of Polaria."

"I mean the ruler of the kingdom to the north
of us—the hidden kingdom of the North Pole,
which is known as Polaria. It is the country Mr.
Andree set out to find—or rather to visit, for that
Swede is a wonderful man, a fine scholar and student, and evidently had some foreknowledge of us
before he started."

"Thank you, Mr. Neerec," returned Alice.
"You are really becoming fascinating! Tell me
more! How large is Polaria?"

"Oh, about twenty times as large as New York
State or England."

"Is it possible?" commented Alice. "I'd no idea there was so much room north of us."

"Really? Then you ought to look at your map," advised Neerec. "You will find that the Polar Basin is a thousand miles in diameter and contains half a million of square miles, so that there would be room there for the inhabitants of France, Germany, Great Britain and the United States!"

"Surprising!" murmured Alice. "I had never looked at the matter in that light. And do you mean to tell me that there exists in the Polar Basin a great country called Polaria?"

"Yes," replied Neerec. "That's the actual truth of the matter."

"What are the inhabitants of this 'Hidden Kingdom' called?"

"Polar Aryans, or Polarians."

"What is their number?"

"About a couple of millions, of whom something like one-fourth reside in the National Capital, which is called Polaria City!"

During these questions and answers Pirr Garvel

had been shifting his weight from one foot to the other, with a constantly increasing uneasiness, and he now swung a chair high above his head, approaching his rival.

"You ought to be killed," he declared, "for betraying these secrets, and you will be, if you ever go back to Polaria."

Turning to Alice he added :

"Pay no further attention to him, Miss Haddon, but let me enlighten you in regard to these matters."

He gave the chair in his hand a flourish that caused his rival to recoil half a dozen yards, and then sat down in it, planting himself in front of the girl and as near to her as possible.

"What is the language of Polaria, Mr. Garvel?" asked Alice, turning upon him a glance especially designed to drive Swib Neerec to desperation.

"It's English," was the reply. "For hundreds and thousands of years we spoke Ayran, which is a good deal like Sanscrit, but we changed the national speech to English about thirty years ago, at the time the Japanese did, and for the same reason that they did!"

"Is it possible!" exclaimed the girl, greatly interested. "Are there any newspapers in Polaria?"

"Yes, one—the *Weekly Gazette*."

"Do you have any dealings with foreign nations?"

"None whatever, nor do we allow them to have any dealings with us, or even acquire the least knowledge of our existence. It's death for anyone to leave our nation or enter it—anyone whomsoever!"

"Why such a law?"

"Because we are all keenly alive to the necessity of keeping our existence a secret!" exclaimed Pirr Garvel. "If the great powers of the earth only knew——"

## CHAPTER XVI.

*Alice Continues to Handle Her Admirers Cleverly.*

PIRR GARVEL hesitated, the more naturally because Swib Neerec had half arisen from his chair, clutching the back of it with a nervousness which constituted a menace.

"If the great powers of the earth only knew?" insinuated Alice, with her most fetching smile.

"Knew what a climate we possess," continued Garvel, "and what resources, what an advanced civilization, what a past and present, what glories and grandeurs—in a word, what charms and beauties are scattered all through the fabric of our lives and dealings—why, they'd come and crowd us off the earth so quick they'd make our heads swim."

"But you have an army," suggested Alice.

"Oh, yes, we have an army, and one up-to-date in equipment," admitted Garvel, "but what could two millions do against hundreds? All history and

experience teach us that the higher forms of civilization go down like froth before superior force,
however brutal and barbarous may be the invaders, and such would be our fate instantly before the
awful avalanche of numbers a discovery of our
kingdom would precipitate upon us."

"But haven't your people—now and then, one
of them—made their way out of Polaria to foreign
countries?"

"Oh, yes.  That has happened three times in
my lifetime," replied Garvel.  "One Polarian made
his way across the 'Icy Barrier' to Russia and
babbled all he knew there, but he was seized and
locked up as an insane man, and soon died in con-
finement.  The second man was a runaway mur-
derer, who kept very still of course, about his native land and its secrets.  As to the third man, he
died within a week after reaching your country, for
about the same reason that a polar bear dies there,
and the little he said about Polaria was regarded
as vagaries and ravings."

"You miserable rascal and traitor, to be telling
all these things!" howled Swib Neerec, darting

forward and throwing his rival to the floor.
" Won't you catch it, if you ever get back to the
kingdom ! Silence ! Not a word, sir ! It's my
turn now."

Seating himself anew in front of Alice, he signi-
fied by his most winsome expression of countenance, that he was ready to make further sacrifices
of his person and fatherland for the sake of getting
into her good graces.

" And did any of our people ever make their way
into Polaria, Mr. Neerec ?" asked Alice.

"Yes," was the reply. " That has also happened.
A couple of sailors arrived at Polaria City a few
years ago in a whaling ship which had entered the
Arctic Ocean at Behring Straits, but they were
well received by our people, married nice girls and
are now contented fathers of families, ranking
among our most prudent and patriotic citizens. A
third man reached us from Baffin's Bay and Greenland—I never knew exactly how—but he was
frozen to death in a desperate attempt to get back
to his home in New England. On one occasion
several shipwrecked whalers made their way to

Polaria by the Spitzbergen route, but they endured such hardships that none of them lived more than two or three years after their arrival."

"And will papa and I be obliged to remain always in Polaria if we once make our way into that country?" asked the girl.

"Of course you will," assured Neerec.

"As a matter of fact, you will never be allowed to retrace the steps you have already taken," assured Pirr Garvel. "The orders we have received deal fully and decisively with that very point."

"Whose house is this?" asked the girl, with a keen look around the apartment.

"It belongs to the Government, and has been in use for many a century, as indeed its aspect would tell you," answered Neerec.

"A sort of border station between you and the outer world, is it not?"

"Exactly. It may indeed be regarded as the 'jumping-off place' for us Polarians, as it is the very last one between us and the 'Polar Pack!'"

In the silence that succeeded there came four irregular tappings upon an outer door, as if the limb of a tree had been blown against it, and the girl comprehended. Those four taps announced the presence of the three Swedes and Mr. Haddon.

"And are balloons common in Polaria, existing in so many styles, sizes and varieties?" resumed the girl.

"Certainly. Any one can have a balloon if he is inclined that way," replied Neerec, "but it's a curious fact that the Polarians are not great travellers —a fact which comes from our necessity for isolation. The screw-balloon, which is Garvel's, and the torpedo-balloon, which is mine, and the ball-balloon, which you haven't seen yet—these are the principal varieties. The latter is the most complete of all, and promises to drive all others out of existence."

"And now I want you both to tell me the truth," said Alice, looking from one to the other. "Mr. Garvel has told me some things, Mr. Neerec, but I want you to confirm and repeat them."

"Certainly," returned Neerec.

"As if we could or would tell you anything but the truth," declared Garvel.

"Are you alone in these solitudes?" continued the girl.

"I am," said Neerec.

"I have my family here, a mother and sister who came here to lighten the burden of my official duties, as life here is a sort of banishment," explained Garvel. "You caught a glimpse of both of them while they were getting our breakfast."

"And who else have you here with you?"

"Only my two men, my engineer and fireman, who have had their breakfast and gone to sleep in my airship."

"And you, sir," pursued Alice, turning to Neerec, "whom have you here with you? Any family?"

"None ; only my two men, who have turned in to make up for being awake all night," was his answer.

"And are you—the eight of you—all the inhabitants in this vicinity?"

"All, Miss Haddon—all within a good many

miles of us," answered Garvel. "This portion of the Basin is considered a sort of No Man's Land, not worth peopling, and where, in fact, a man would have a pretty hard task to get a living, except in those seasons of the year when there is good hunting and fishing."

"There is a straggling outlaw or two somewhere in this neighborhood—no one knows just where," observed Neerec, "but they will take good care not to intrude upon us or any one else, for fear of being taken back to Polaria for punishment."

Alice looked the two men over again. Certainly they were a very peculiar couple, and she did not by any means flatter herself that she had found out all that was to be known about them.

"How long have your people known," she resumed, "that Mr. Andree intended to explore these regions by means of his balloon?"

"Oh, for a long time."

"And what did they think about it?"

"They were filled with terror, fearing that all sorts of misfortunes would come to them in case Andree were to succeed in his purpose."

" What sort of misfortunes ?"

" Why, the advent of the Great Powers in our
midst, the seizure of our territory, the destruction
of our Government, the appropriation of our gold
—in a word, our utter annihilation as a people !"

" And were any measures taken to head off Mr.
Andree ?" demanded the girl, with an anxiety she
sought vainly to conceal.

" Yes, a good many," avowed Neerec.   " To begin with, our people received warning everywhere
to be on the lookout for the expected intrusion,
and to report any and every development at head-
quarters at the earliest possible moment."

" What else ?"

" Well, Garvel and I received word that promo-
tion would be given us if we could either capture
Andree and his party, or report that their expedition had come to a disastrous end."

" Which signifies a report that they had ceased
to be dangerous ?"

" Exactly !  The desire of our authorities is to
hear of them dead rather than to hear of them living," sai i Garvel.

"Were you empowered to assassinate the explorers?"

"Yes, in case of their going too far, and becoming too much of a peril for our Government and people," confessed Pirr Garvel.

"Of which necessity you were to be the judges?"

"Yes, that's the truth of the matter."

"But this doesn't seem to me to be the policy of an enlightened government," protested Alice.

"Perhaps not," admitted Garvel, "but it is the policy of a government which knows what dire consequences will follow if the 'enlightened' nations of the earth once get a footing among us."

"Have you two been occupying this place in concert and harmony?"

"No; Garvel is boss here," confessed Neerec with a sigh. "The spot fixed for my residence is, as I've said, fifty miles from here. In fact, I have no business to come here, and would hardly have found my way here if I hadn't been guided here by Mr. Andree's balloon."

" What! That's how you came here ?" cried Pirr Garvel, leaping to his feet, " Rascal !"

" Rascal to yourself !" retorted Neerec. " For a fortnight past, or ever since you met Miss Haddon, you have been dodging me, and telling me all sorts of lies to prevent me from discovering her existence and whereabouts. But I am now as well posted and planted as yourself ——"

" Peace, my friends," interrupted the girl, with an authoritative flourish of the hand. " I must warn you both against having any quarrel about me, or in my presence. The truth is, I am not at your mercy, nor in any sense your captive. My father and Mr. Andree are at hand, prepared to protect me and themselves, and I now have the pleasure of presenting them to you."

Raising her voice, she called :

" Come in, all of you !" and the three Swedes and Mr. Haddon entered accordingly.

## CHAPTER XVII.

*The Explorer's Definite Triumph over All the Difficulties of the Route—Off for Polaria!*

WITH what joy the good clergyman enfolded Alice in his arms will be understood without the telling ; yet the earnest and ever-present trust of both of them in the goodness and mercy of God had enabled them to wait for this moment with a calmness and patience approaching serenity.

" I knew we should have you again, dearest," was the greeting of Mr. Haddon, as he kissed her tenderly.

" And have you noted all I have been saying and doing, papa ?"

" All," he answered, passing her on to Andree.

For one moment the young couple seemed to hesitate as to the nature and form of their greeting, and then they rushed into each other's arms clinging to and caressing one another as if they had been friends of a lifetime,

"Oh! It has been such an awful trial—this separation!" confessed Alice, burying her face in Andree's bosom.

"I should have died but for the hope of finding you," declared the explorer. "Never, never again shall anything come between us while the breath of life is in me!"

"Never! never!" affirmed Alice. "We——"

She was interrupted by a wild cry of dismay from Dr. Strindberg, who had walked to the door.

"Heavens! See there!" he cried, with outstretched hand.

One glance was enough. Every eye took in the sinister turn which had been given to the situation. The four men in charge of the two airships had been aroused by the advent of the exploring party and had hastened to get up steam and take their departure, so that they were already miles distant.

"And this leaves us in a fine situation!" growled Fraenckel, who was usually the first to comment upon severe surprises. "For how long are you provisioned, Mr. Garvel?"

"For a few weeks, more or less, according to

our number, and the amount of game we can pick up around us."

"Then we need not despair," commented Andree. "I suppose there is an overland route into Polaria ?"

"Yes, overland and over water."

"Then we'll get there just the same, with or without airships," declared the explorer. "As the next measure, Mr. Garvel, my friends and I will have to constitute ourselves your guests to the extent of a breakfast."

"With pleasure," responded Garvel, touching a bell. "You shall be amply served in a few minutes."

This matter of the breakfast had scarcely been attended to, when the doctor came hurrying into the house in the wildest excitement.

"Another airship is in sight," he reported. "It is close at hand, and coming here !"

There was a general rush for the door, but Strindberg intercepted everybody, waving them back.

"Not a step !" he cried. "We mustn't show

ourselves.    If the airship calls here we must seize it."

His companions assented to this suggestion, it was so essentially the proper suggestion to act upon at that moment.

"Will you come here, Mr. Garvel," pursued the doctor, "and take a secret glance at the stranger ?"

The captain complied, starting violently.

"It's a ball-balloon !" he cried, his face paling. "I recognize it !   It's a dispatch boat in the service of the Government !   It's coming here for some important purpose !"

"Indeed !" cried Andree.   "How many men are there likely to be on it ?"

"Not more than three—the officer in charge and his engineer and fireman."

The doctor looked out again, making a rapid survey of the airship, which was now barely a couple of miles distant.

"We shall need her for the completion of our journey to the Pole," said Strindberg, "and hence we will seize her !"

"No !  No !  You can't do that !" protested

Neerec excitedly. "For any such act as that the punishment will be death! Such an act is equivalent to 'piracy on the high seas,' you know!"

"I can't help that," decided Andree, without an instant's hesitation. "We all are out for Polaria and intend to get there! The next thing in hand is to lay out the measures to be taken!"

A plan of action was promptly elaborated, beginning with the seizure and binding of the two captives, and then the explorer turned anew to his prisoners.

"I see that this 'ball-balloon,'" he said, "is so called because it has two balls in the places occupied, in Garvel's ship by the aluminum screws!"

The two men assented.

"But is it by those two balls that the weight of the airship is supported?"

"Yes, such is indeed the case," answered Neerec.

"But they seem very small for the work required of them," said Andree.

"They are small—certainly not more than five feet in diameter," responded Neerec. "But they are filled with a gas several thousand times lighter than air—a gas made from that found in the bones of the eider duck. Being so much lighter than the air, this new article has, even in small quantities, a lifting power that is surprising."

At the end of a few minutes, after the prisoners had been concealed, the strange airship had reached the earth, and the officer in command, after two or three calls had been left unanswered was heard approaching rapidly the entrance of the dwelling.

"Are you here, Garvel?" he demanded, halting in the doorway.

"I am here," said Andree, stepping into view from the adjacent room. "Whom have I the honor of addressing?"

"I am Captain Stobeck, of the royal navy," was the answer, as the officer produced a formidable looking paper, "and I have been sent here with orders for the instant execution of Herr Andree and his associates wherever we may catch them. Who are you, sir?"

"I'll tell you in a moment, captain," replied

Andree, with a gesture that caused his fellow-explorers to hurry into the room. "Now, then!"

It's needless to say that Capt. Stobeck made a desperate resistance to the attack of which he instantly became the object, but his efforts were useless, and within a few moments he had been overpowered and bound securely.

"What does this violence mean?" he then demanded.

"It means that I am the 'Herr Andree,' your government has ordered to be executed at sight," replied the explorer calmly. "It also means that you will remain here with Garvel and Neerec, while I and my friends take charge of your airship and proceed to Polaria City!"

"You will?" gasped the helpless official.

"We certainly shall, sir!"

For one brief moment the captain looked consternated, and then a laugh worthy of a demon escaped him.

"All right!" he cried. "Push on! I wish you joy!"

Securing the three men in a stone cellar, which made an excellent prison, it being supplied with stout bolts and locks, Andree led the way to the spot where the ball-balloon was lying, explaining in a few words to the men in charge of it the radical change which had taken place in the situation.

"You will steam back to Polaria City as soon as you can," finished the explorer, with smiling serenity, "only you will have us for passengers and commander instead of Capt. Stobeck."

"But who is to release the captain and his friends from the cellar?" asked the engineer.

"Oh, Garvel's wife and daughter. The task will not be an easy one, but they can accomplish it by the time we are fairly started on our journey."

In a few minutes more the new passengers had taken their places, the airship had been put afloat. and was advancing northward at a speed of half a mile a minute.

"And isn't this fine?" cried the explorer, looking around upon his companions, while Alice

nestled lovingly beside her father.  " This may be
regarded as our definite departure for the land of
our dreams and of the world's long dreaming!
We are off for Polaria !"

## CHAPTER XVIII.

*The Explorers Getting New Light upon Their*
*Situation.*

A FEW minutes were naturally given to the rejoicings inseparable from such an occasion, and then
the explorer turned his attention to his engineer
and fireman, the former of whom was steering their
ball-balloon.

"You will excuse me, I hope," he said, "for having pressed you into our service with so little cere-
mony ?"

"Oh, don't mention it, ' returned the engineer,
good-naturedly.   "We leave all that for you to ar-
range with our superiors, begining with Stobeck
and ending with the King.  We don't find any
fault with you, Mr. Andree ; do we, Hooger ?"

"Not any, Birep," affirmed the fireman.

"You have plenty of fuel for the voyage, I suppose ?" continued Andree.

" Plenty, sir."

" In what direction are you steering ?"

" Due north."

" And how long will it take us to arrive at Polaria City ?" .

" A few hours only, as we are now going at a
thirty-mile clip."

The explorer gave his attention a few moments
to the working of the machinery employed for the
propelling of the craft, and was loud in his praise
of it, the engine occupying very little space, the fuel
being a few gallons of oil, and the lifting power of
the balls so thoroughly under control that the balloon could be placed upon any desired plane,
whether close to the earth or hundreds or thousands
of feet in the air.

" Have you ever been at the North Pole ?—at the
exact spot where latitude ends ?" resumed Andree.

" Oh, yes, more times than you have fingers and
toes," replied Birep.

" Hundreds of times," affirmed Hooger.

" And what did you find there ?"

" The nicest little country there is in the world,

with open water on three sides of it—in a word,
Polaria, an island which is large enough to be
termed a continent, its northern shores covering
the Pole, and its southern reaching down to the
Arctic archipelago of North America."

"What sort of a country?" asked Strindberg.

"A country," replied Birep, "that would remind
you a good deal of Switzerland, as seen from
the railway most anywhere between Berne and
Geneva."

"Ah! you have been there?" demanded Alice.

"I have," replied the engineer, flushing nervously, "but my betrayal of the fact was quite un-
intentional."

"I comprehend what sort of a country you
mean," said the explorer. "It is one where Arctic
peaks capped with snow and ice can be seen from
the same point where your gaze rests upon grass,
herbs and flowers."

"That's it, exactly," said Birep. "And in the
midst of this radiant landscape, on the shore of a
deep, broad bay, almost enclosed by two long prom-
montories, is one of the handsomest cities ever

built by man, with a population of a quarter of a million—Polaria City !"

" Isn't it cold there ?"

" It was at one time, but we changed all that some thousands of years ago."

" How changed it ?"

" Why, the early fathers of our race opened great borings into the earth, many of which ranged from two to six miles in depth, and thus brought the internal heat of the earth to the surface. We have no other heat than that—no other fuel. The whole country of Polaria—the ' Volcano Kingdom,' as we call it—is a man-made country ; a country wherein man has struggled with Nature and overcome it ; where Arctic ice and snow have been replaced by tropical heat; where whole oceans have been thawed out and turned into delightful summer seas; a country, in short, which is warmed throughout by the volcanic fires below, precisely as you warm your houses in Gothenburg from the stoves in the basement."

The explorers, including Mr. Haddon and Alice,

held their breath at this statement, it was at once
so new and so striking.

This " Volcano Kingdom," this man-made country which had been wrested from Jack Frost—this
must certainly be, they all thought, one of the wonders of the ages.

" But you must see it for yourselves before you
can form any just idea of it," said Birep.   " Fortunately it will not be long before you make its acquaintance."

The discussion that succeeded lasted several
hours, ending only with the serving of a fine colla-
tion by Hooger.

" We're getting on, you see, and will soon be at
our destination," remarked Andree, lighting a cigar.
" And in the meantime," he added, producing a few
printed pages from one of his pockets, " here is the
extract I proposed to read to you yesterday,
just before the cry of Miss Haddon for assistance came up from the wreck to us.   Let me now
carry out my purpose and read it.   The article
from which I am making this extract appeared in
*Scribner's*, volume ix, page 477.   It is entitled :

'Where the Ice Never Melts,' and was written by
Robert Gordon Butler.  Here are the points to
which I wish to call your attention."

Settling himself comfortably into the recumbent
posture he had taken, he began reading the following statement :

" ' Years ago, in 1876, thirteen whalers were
caught in the ice-pack.  Every effort was made to
break out, but in vain ; the vessels were firmly fas-
tened in the ice, and all the time the Arctic current
was steadily carrying them further and further into
the North.  They were eighty miles in the pack ;
eighty miles of ice were between them and the open
water ; so it was decided to abandon the ships.' "

" As we ought to have abandoned our balloon
before it drifted across Spitzbergen," growled
Fraenckel.  " But go on."

Andree resumed reading :

" ' But three men did not wish to leave the vessels.  They were comfortable ; the ships were safe ;
they were in no danger ; they would not leave.  So
the captains and their crews departed, and only
three men were left to man the thirteen vessels.'

" ' For two days the refugees toiled over the un-
even ice, over hummocks, around leads, launching
their boats when necessary, making slow progress,
but always getting nearer and nearer to the open
water.   On the third day two of the captains be-
thought them of valuable furs left behind on their
vessels, and, knowing that they could rejoin their
friends again, they decided to return to their ships
and recover them.   So they left them, and in a single day passed over what the fugitives had needed
two days to cover.'

" ' As they drew near the vessels a feeling of awe
came over them.   The ships were so still, so lonely
there, in the great ice-field, that it seemed almost
wicked to board them, to disturb their quiet in any
way. The captains descended into the cabin. Worn
out by the day's long march, excited by the strangeness of their surroundings, the sight that met them
was a shock.  In the captain's stove burned a bright
fire ; over it hissed a kettle, and before it, book in
hand, and looking up over his spectacles at the intruders, sat comfortably the steward of the vessel
while the other two men sat by smoking.' "

The interest of the listeners had deepened to breathlessness, there was so much in their own situation and circumstances to give effect to the narrative. The explorer cleared his throat and continued :

" ' The steward did the honors of his habitation ; the captains took supper with him and slept in warm beds. In the morning he urged them to stay ; they begged him to return. Neither was convinced, and at last the captains departed with their furs, leaving the steward in his comfortable quarters, and started back after the weary train in the middle of the great ice-field. Often, while in sight of the fleet, they turned and looked at it, and thought of the lonely occupants of the lonely vessels. Each time they looked the vessels were visible less distinctly ; and at last, when they looked, they could see nothing but the still, cold fields of white ice.' "

"From that day to this no human being has seen aught of those thirteen vessels, with their lonely crews. In the heart of the great ice-field— ice that never melts—lie the vessels; and in one of them sit the steward and his companions, waiting for the coming of a captain greater than he who interrupted them twice seven years ago."

The silence that succeeded for a few moments resembled stupefaction.

"Why, that steward must have had an idea," then commented Fraenckel. "He must have thought that his frozen fleet would drift across the Pole!"

"He certainly did," assured Andree. "Does not Butler say, in so many words, that 'all the time the Arctic current was stealthily carrying them further and further into the North?' That steward was a believer in the existence of the current which is ever sweeping across the North Pole from Behring Straits to Greenland."

"And what can have become of those three men and thirteen ships?" asked Fraenckel.

"I believe we shall see or hear more about them before this voyage is ended," answered Andree, restoring the printed pages to his pocket. "In fact, I shouldn't be surprised to see them."

"You wouldn't?" queried Birep, looking up with a strange smile.

" No, sir."

"Then look from either of those windows on our port bow."

All hastened to act upon this suggestion, and Birep added :

" There they are !"

## CHAPTER XIX.

*The Frozen Fleet—In Sight of Polaria City.*

ONE glance was enough!

The thirteen ships so strangely given over to decay and destruction were indeed within a mile of the explorers!

"Just where those three men drifted in them all these years ago," explained Birep.

With what interest the explorers looked upon this startling apparition from the past need not be stated.

"And the three men ?" asked the doctor.

" Two of them are dead, but the third is still living among us," replied Hooger.

The masts and yards of the thirteen ships were more or less broken and missing, and their sails hung in tatters or were altogether absent. Many of their taffrails and bulwarks had been destroyed, and their decks in several places had rotted away or been torn up for the lumber in them.

"Of course, they would have filled and sunk years ago if our people had not pumped them out often and otherwise cared for them," continued the engineer. " They are used for storage and fishing stations, and even as dwellings. Ah, there is a number of our people in sight upon them !"

The interest with which the explorers gazed upon these strangers can be imagined.

"And that is Polaria," cried Alice, the first to find voice.

"Yes, that is Polaria, its easternmost shore in this direction," replied Birep. "From this time onward you will not lose sight of it."

"And what country is that we have left behind us?" demanded Strindberg, continuing to look out upon the scene beneath him.

"It isn't a country, it's an island," replied Birep. "It's about twenty miles in diameter, and may contain three hundred square miles. It owes its verdure, its forests, and other aspects, including its river—which is only an arm of the sea—to the fact that the Gulf Stream pockets in front of it, and that it is also a centre of volcanic disturbance."

"Does it belong to Polaria?"

"In the modern political sense of 'belonging'— yes!" replied Hooger, smiling. "In other terms, our people have occupied it several centuries as an outpost and place of banishment."

"Has the Island any name?"

"Certainly.  It is called Mastodon Island, from a herd of mastodons which have descended from a single pair stranded there two or three hundred years ago, according to popular belief."

"Are there any inhabitants on Mastodon Island?" asked Fraenckel, as Andree sat the picture of amazement.

"Only those you have seen there."

"And who really is Pirr Garvel?"

"He's Prince Ardeb, the only son and heir of the King of Polaria."

"A Prince? The Crown Prince?" exclaimed Mr. Haddon.

The engineer assented.

"Then what is he doing there?" cried the doctor.

"He has been exiled for three years for refusing to marry the Princess selected for him by his father."

Alice and Andree exchanged meaning glances. Here was certainly a curious complication in one of the principal features of their situation.

"Who is the woman I saw at Garvel's?" asked Alice,

" She's his old nurse, who has voluntarily accompanied him.

" And Erba ?"

" She's the nurse's daughter."

" Neither is related to him ?"

" No, sir.  The Prince has a sister, the Princess Rubal, but she has never left Polaria."

" Is this sister single ?" pursued Alice.

" Yes, for the reason that the kingdom does not contain a suitable match for her."

" Is she beautiful ?"

" As a dream, and she is also finely educated," declared Birep.

Alice Haddon looked up quickly, losing color, so easy was it to foresee that this state of affairs might readily lead up to serious trouble.  With the Prince Ardeb, alias Pirr Garvel, so violently in love with her, and the Princess Rubal in a mood to conceive a violent passion for the explorer, it would be perfectly natural for their advent into Polaria to also be a plunge into trouble.

" And who is Neerec ?" asked Strindberg, seeing

that the young couple were temporarily lost in their reflections.

"He's Prince Volpan, the King's brother, and hence, the uncle of Prince Ardeb."

Despite all her courage, Alice Haddon became still paler at this information.

"What a fatality! That we should be drawn into such relations with these two Princes!" she murmured.

"And that we should have left the pair of them shut up in a cellar like malefactors!" exclaimed Andree.

"How odd, too, that the uncle and nephew should both fall in love with me at first sight!" pursued Alice. "What will be the end of these complications? Something unpleasant, I'm sure!"

"Oh, not necessarily," assured Andree, bending nearer, his face aglow with the tender respect and affection he had conceived for the clergyman's daughter. "They are both in disgrace, you must remember—both banished from court, and it's more than likely they'll have no power to harm us."

"But what has Prince Volpan done that he should be banished to Mastodon Island?" asked Mr. Haddon.

"Well," replied Birep, "he's the head of a so-called liberal or progressive party, which has long been clamoring against the King's policy of silence and exclusion, and has for its platform the opening of Polaria to the knowledge and commerce of the whole world. In fact, Prince Volpan has allowed his zeal to carry him so far that he headed a sort of revolt a year ago, and was, in due course arrested and banished to Mastodon Island for a number of years, I've forgotten just how many."

"And has he no household?" inquired the doctor.

"None, save the two men who assist him in handling his torpedo balloon, which is also his residence. He was very lucky to get that much consideration shown him, as he aimed at nothing less than the dethronement of his brother."

"And these are the men we have affronted so terribly," exclaimed Fraenckel. "Will they not get back at us in some unpleasant fashion?"

"Oh, they are not so innocent as you might suppose," advised Birep. "Both have been offered a full pardon and permission to return to Polaria, if they could furnish proofs of your death."

"Ah, is that why they were on the lookout for me?" demanded the explorer.

"That is certainly one reason why they were placing themselves in touch with you."

"Well, it's a very pretty situation, as it stands," declared Andree, with a broad smile of contentment. "Instead of having the pleasure of reporting our death, the two princes will hear, sooner or later, of our arrival—very much alive—at Polaria City. But what about Stobeck? Was he really sent to Mastodon Island to kill us?"

"He was, sir. Such were the orders given him by Prime Minister Sabat. The fact is, Mr. Andree, your expected advent has shaken both parties to their foundations, the Conservatives being in mortal terror, and the Progressives hoping great things of your coming. To make an end of this violent agitation, Minister Sabat could think of nothing better than to make an end of you, sir."

"I know—'reasons of state,'" commented Andree, his smile deepening. "But how differently things are turning out from what might have been expected. Instead of tamely dying at the orders of Minister Sabat, I am on my way to beard him and his monarch in their capital."

"Heaven be with us," prayed the Rev. Mr. Haddon, as was his wont in critical situations. "If any man ever had danger before him, and wrath behind him, Mr. Andree, you are certainly that man."

"And now, look out and tell me what you see, all of you," enjoined Birep, his strange smile returning.

All hastened to comply.

"Ah, great heavens? What is that I see?" cried Andree, pale with excitement.

"What you see is Polaria City," replied Birep, "the Golden City of the Pole!"

## CHAPTER XX.

### *A New World and a New Race.*

AT a desk in his reception-room in the midst of his palace, sat King Polaris XLVII., the eight hundred and thirty-third monarch in a direct line from the founder of his dynasty, Aryon the Great.

King Polaris looked like a man of middle age, his hair and beard being only slightly sprinkled with gray, but he was in his one hundred and eighteenth year, and in the seventy-fourth of his reign.

"More petitions for Ardeb and Volpan!" he ejaculated, pitching them into a casket resembling a barrel, which stood at the end of his desk. "They'll have to wait awhile. That precious brother of mine hasn't written me yet that he is sorry for having been a demagogue, and Ardeb seems to have forgotten to write at all."

The King's brow became corrugated a few moments, as if he were not at all pleased with the situation of affairs in regard to the absent ones, but his frowns were dissipated by the entrance of his only daugher, the Princess Rubal, a beautiful girl of twenty-three or twenty-four years.

"Oh, I do hope, papa, you will let uncle and brother come back," she declared, throwing her arms around his neck and caressing him.

"And why should they come back, if you please?" demanded the monarch, returning her caresses with all a father's love and admiration.

"Oh, as a matter of policy," replied Rubal, "or as a gracious expression of the royal clemency with which Polaris the Forty-seventh has ever treated his subjects."

"But your uncle would have dethroned me."

"Well, he couldn't have done anything of the kind, papa," declared Rubal. "You are too firmly enthroned in the hearts of your subjects. Besides, you must remember that Uncle Volpan went into that business because his daughter, my cousin, was always belaboring him in that direction, as the result of inordinate ambition. I shouldn't wonder if she has the hope of some day being Queen of Polaria."

"I am well aware that some of the Progressives hope to make use of her in such a way as that," returned the monarch, " but it will be several years before they succeed in their purpose. Your cousin was here yesterday to plead for her father, but I told her we'd leave him awhile longer at Mastodon Island to work out a further problem or two respecting the application of the lifting power of the balls to Crona's balloon."

"Well, papa, whatever you do or decide to do will be right and noble, as always," assured Rubal, caressing him again, " and you know my thanks and approbation, as worthless as they are, will ever accompany your every decision in this or any other matter."

" Rubal is a dear, good girl," muttered the monarch, looking after her as she vanished with a lightness and grace peculiarly her own. "And to think that I cannot find a husband for her—that she is still unmarried. How to change this state of things is now the problem. I must bring some

sort of remedy to this vexatious point within the
next few weeks, certain."

Arousing himself with a shiver, the monarch
raised his voice and called sharply :

" Sinjib !"

" Here, sire," responded a tall and stately servitor, advancing into view from behind a curtain of
richly embroidered tapestry, which covered an
alcove at one side of the apartment.

" Turn on more heat, Sinjib," ordered the monarch. " The place is as cold as an iceberg !"

The man stepped to an immense register at one
end of the room and opened it wide ; then glancing at the thermometer, " The heat here is up to
our average, sire," he announced. " Just eighty-
eight !"

" It must be, then, that my years are telling
upon me," said the King, with a sigh. " I'm afraid
such is the case, Sinjib ! I'm not feeling half as
well as I used to feel fifty or sixy years ago ! All
these troubles with Ardeb and the rest have di-
minished my vitality."

" Your Majesty had better spend another day in

the Silver Grotto," advised Sinjib, with the freedom
and affection of a lifelong friend and servant.
" The magnetism we get there to-day is better than
ever. The north magnetic pole of the south has
changed a fifth of a degree very abruptly since the
last report, and the consequence is that the stream
of electricity pouring upon us from the cosmic
regions is better and purer than ever. Your Majesty must try it !"

" I will, Sinjib ; I will," said the King, with another sigh. " Unless I take better care of myself
I shall never see my third century."

He dropped into his chair, remaining a few moments in an attitude of dejection, but soon aroused
himself.

" Bring me the latest copies of the New York
*World* and London *Times*," he ordered. " I want
to see if those infernal great powers of Europe
are carrying on as usual. Have you read the papers yourself, Sinjib ?"

" I have, Your Majesty."

" And what is the prospect of war in Europe or
Asia ? Is it sure to come, and coming quickly ?"

"I'm afraid not, sire," answered Sinjib, laying upon his master's desk the newspapers demanded. "The black and threatening cloud which has so long hovered over Europe is still in a state of hovering, in my humble estimation."

"In mine, too, Sinjib," growled the monarch, testily. "Curse them! I wish they'd begin fighting at once and keep it up until there was nothing left of them but a dim tradition! In such a case as that we might hope to keep our existence here concealed a while longer. By the way, have you any further news respecting Andree?"

"Nothing more, sire," replied Sinjib. "The very latest was that he left Dane's Island at 2.30 P.M. on the 11th of July, but was driven back to Spitzbergen, and there is even a report in the *Gazette* office that his balloon has dropped into the ocean!"

"I only hope it has, Sinjib," declared the king. "That man has been such a nightmare to me that I'd like to find relief from him. Were those orders to the princes concerning him duly delivered to them?"

"They were, sire, and both will surely be on the lookout, night and day, for him."

"They understand that they can come back here if they can bring me proofs of his death?"

"They do, sire—that is the condition your Majesty was pleased to announce to Prime Minister Sabat."

"Well, let them get away with that Swede—I care not by what process—and I shall be glad to see them back in my capital. In the meantime. Sinjib—but what is that noise in the streets and in front of the palace?"

"I'll go and see, sire."

The old servitor hastened from the reception-room, but was soon back again, his cheeks rosy with haste and excitement.

"The great central crater is again in a state of eruption, sire," he reported, "and the Royal Cosmographer says that seven cubic miles of melted rock will be irrupted over Eider rocks and vicinity before this time to-morrow."

"Well, let her irrupt," said the monarch, shivering again. "But surely that mob in the street

cannot be so excited and noisy about a few square
miles, more or less, of melted rock.   What else is
behind this brawling ?"

"Well, sire, the ball-balloon of Capt. Stobeck is
returning from Mastodon Island."

"Ah, glorious !  This quick return speaks well
for the success of the captain's mission !  Bring him
to me as soon as he lands.   His orders are to come
direct to the palace.   Go and fetch him to me."

## CHAPTER XXI.

*Arrival of Andree at Polaria City—Tremendous Excitement of the Polarians.*

SINJIB hurried from the room, but came back after a couple of minutes at a much quicker pace than he had used in leaving it.

"The captain is not there, sire," he reported with an agitation he could not conceal. "His ship is occupied by strangers!"

"By strangers?"

The monarch dropped again into the chair from which he had arisen, and sat as if annihilated.

"By strangers?" repeated the king. "What sort of strangers?"

"Well, the foremost is a man with a white necktie—a man of clerical aspect and with a clerical countenance—a man who is clerical all over, and who is doubtless a clergyman——"

"Ach! Gott im Himmel! It's the old, old

story!" interrupted the monarch, becoming so white and looking so helpless that Sinjib hastened to hold a vial of salts to his nostrils. "It's an invasion by the English! An invasion in their regular form and in accordance with their regular system. First they send out a missionary to indoctrinate the heathen; then they send a consul to look after the missionary, and at last they send an army to look after the consul. Oh, curse them! Go and get further particulars."

Sinjib made another hasty visit to the steps of the palace, returning more excited than ever.

"There's a woman with them," he reported; a young and beautiful woman."

"Oh, of course, *Cherchez la femme !*" roared the monarch. "But there are women and women, and this may be one of the right kind. Beautiful is she?"

"As an angel, it seems to me, sire, as far as I can judge at this distance."

"Perhaps she'll do for a bride for Ardeb, if she's well born," muttered the monarch. "Needless to say, she'll never leave Polaria alive, be she good or evil.   Who else is in the ship, Sinjib?"

"No less than three men, sire, in addition to the clergyman."

"Three, Sinjib?   Oh, *merveilles celestes !*   A regular army of invasion !   Is the ship headed directly for the palace?"

"It is, sire !"

"But about the three men, Sinjib?" resumed the monarch hastily.   "What are they like ?   English, do you think?"

"No, sire ; they look more like—like Swedes !"

"Like Swedes, Sinjib!" cried Polaris.   "Ah, you stab me to the heart."

"The truth before all else, sire—such have ever been the orders of your royal majesty."

"True ! true !   Speak freely."

"Well, sire, I think the three men with the girl and missionary are Swedes, and the very three Swedes who left Dane's Island three days ago. "

"Oh, no—no !" protested the monarch.

"The truth, sire, the truth before all else !   And

one of the three men, I have no doubt, is Andree himself."

The monarch uttered a gasping cry, started as if unable to speak, but he promptly aroused himself by a desperate effort.

"Andree himself!" he repeated. "And coming here in the very ship in which Stobeck sailed to intercept him? What a state of things! And what of Stobeck? Has he shown himself or made any signals?"

"No, sire, but I caught glimpses of both Hooger and Birep so that we can have no doubt of the identity of the ship with that of the captain."

"And the captain not visible?" muttered the King. "Well, our cloud, Sinjib, which has been hovering so long, has now ceased to hover, and is descending in one deadly swoop upon us! If that man is Andree——"

"Oh, he's Andree, sire; depend upon it," assured Sinjib, as his royal master paused from sheer want of breath. "I recognized him from the photos we have sent out all over the country."

The King took one long look at his faithful ser-

vitor to assure himself that he had heard aright,
and then drew himself up firmly in his chair,
gathering his mantle of furs around him.

"Bring them all here," he ordered ; "missionary,
girl and all—even to Hooger and Birep! I must
learn at once the meaning of these sinister develop.
ments. Go and bring the newcomers here, keeping everybody else out and closing and locking all
the doors behind you."

"Yes, sire."

"Moreover, tell the captains of the guards to
keep the palace grounds cleared of every sort of
intruder," added the monarch. "No passage in or
out to any human being except these newcomers,
until further orders."

"Please except me, papa," pleaded the Princess
Rubal, appearing at the inner entrance, "I—I wish
to be near you, papa, on such an exciting occasion
as this."

"Come along, puss," invited the King, the ghost
of a smile illuminating his visage for one brief moment at the sight of her gracious beauty. "Take

your place here on this hassock and note well all that is about to be said and done here."

He waved his hand imperiously to Sinjib, who hastened to acquit himself of the duties which had been confided to him.

For two or three minutes the tumult and excitement in front of the palace seemed greater than ever, but it then began to lessen rapidly, under the energetic action of the guards, and was soon followed by a silence little short of sinister, as Sinjib reappeared at the head of the little band of invaders.

"Mr. Andree, the famous explorer, sire," announced Sinjib, by way of introduction, indicating by a gesture the foremost of the newcomers.

## CHAPTER XXII.

*Andree and King Polaris—-the Monarch Inquires into the Proceedings of the Invaders.*

FEARLESS and unabashed, his manly face glowing with honor and honesty, his attitude one of profound respect for the monarch—self-possessed and self-confiding, a hero in the highest sense of the term—such was Explorer Andree at the moment Sinjib ushered him into the presence of his royal master.

"Speak, Swede!" was all Polaris could say, so greatly was he puzzled and disturbed by this extraordinary influx of so many strangers into his dominions.

Ere another word could be uttered, however, the captain of the royal guards appeared at the entrance by which the explorer and his party had reached the King's presence.

"If it please Your Majesty," said the newcomer,

inclining himself profoundly, " His Excellency,
Premier Sabat, desires admittance to the royal
presence, having important communications to
offer."

" Let him come in," replied the King, and Sabat
entered accordingly, saluting his royal master with
the humblest inclination of which his somewhat
ancient frame was capable.

" Sit down, Sabat," enjoined the monarch, ac-
knowledging with a slight nod the greeting of his
distinguished subject.

" By Your Majesty's most gracious leave, then,"
said the Premier, laying his hand upon a chair, and
advancing it a few yards, " I will place myself between Your Majesty and this terrible intruder."

His air and manner were of a scornful and
threatening character, not to speak of them as presenting a formal accusation, as he took possession
of the chair offered him, and turned his cold, gray
eyes upon the explorer and his companions.

" You are aware, then, are you, Sabat, who this
man is ?" inquired the King, indicating Andree.

" I am, Your Majesty—only too well aware of his

identity and of the crimes of which he has been guilty since invading Your Majesty's dominions."

" Crimes, Sabat ?"

" That's the word I used, sire," declared the Premier, " and I beg to repeat it. Your Majesty is already aware, I believe, that this man sailed away in his balloon from Dane's Island——"

" Oh, yes ; I am aware of that departure, which is now a matter of ancient history," interrupted the King impatiently. "What we are anxious to know is simply why he has appeared in our presence under these extraordinary surroundings."

" I am here to make all these things as plain as day," returned the minister. " This man and his party reached Mastodon Island at an early hour this morning, where they made an assault upon the two princes, capturing them and shutting them up in the cellar of the government station and leaving them for dead."

" Nonsense," commented Andree, breaking in upon the ominous silence that succeeded. " The Princes are in no wise injured. As a matter of fact, I had no fight with them. I simply invited them to constitute themselves my prisoners and they did so."

" Without drawing a weapon ?" questioned the King.

"Without offering the least resistance of any kind, Your Majesty," declared Andree.

" And you bound them with ropes, did you ?"

" I had to do so, sire, in order to have them out of the way before the arrival of Captain Stobeck."

" Then you had seen him approaching in his ball-balloon ?"

" I had, sire."

" And you also took him prisoner, did you ?"

"As in duty bound, sire," admitted Andree, " but I have the pleasure of reporting that he fought like a tiger."

" But you were too much for him ?"

" Naturally, the three of us."

He indicated Fraenckel and Strindberg by a gesture, taking a step or two to one side to uncover them fully to the gaze of the monarch.

" What are their names ?" inquired the King, after a brief examination of the faces and figures before him, in which the Princess Rubal seemed to take as much interest as he did.

The explorer mentioned them, and the monarch resumed :

" And so you three laid violent hands upon Stobeck, did you, as also upon the Princes ?"

" We did, sire !" acknowledged Andree.

" And left them shut up in the cellar ?"

" Naturally, but we were ignorant of the identity of the Princes until after we left Mastodon Island."

" And how did you discover who they really are ?"

" Birep and Hooger told us during the journey hither.  We encountered Prince Ardeb soon after leaving Dane's Island, and had quite a conversation with him, in the course of which he said that his name was Pirr Garvel."

" I know why he took that course," said the King.  " He is under strict orders not to reveal his identity to anybody during the period of his banishment."

" As to Prince Volpan, we met him late yester-

day afternoon, and had with him quite a conversation, in the course of which he said that his name
was Swib Neerec," explained Andree.   "Your
Majesty will see from this statement that we were
wholly ignorant of the identity of the Princes at
the moment we felt called upon to take them prisoners."

"And what is to become of them?" asked the
King.   "Who is to release them after your departure?"

"The nurse and her daughter."

"Were they in any way injured in the struggle
you had with them?"

"I beg your Majesty's pardon," replied Andree,
"but we had no struggle with the Princes.   They
saw at a glance that they hadn't the ghost of a
chance for any resistance they could offer to be
successful."

"But Stobeck?   Wasn't he a good deal battered
and bruised before he surrendered?"

"I'm afraid he was, sire," answered the explorer.
"I can only speak in the highest praise of him."

"But what was the motive of your attack on Stobeck?"

"Why, Your Majesty, it was a case of eat or be eaten! He told us he had received orders to put me to death at sight, and I experienced a natural objection to any such proceeding."

The King frowned severely, but it was evident that his respect for the explorer was of a very pronounced character.

"Another thing, sire," resumed Andree, "we had lost our balloon, and I had to seize that of Stobeck as the only possible method of continuing my journey to Your Majesty's capital."

"But where were the balloons of the Princes?"

"The engineers and firemen in charge of them had run away with them."

The frown which had flashed across the royal brow from time to time appeared, at this declaration, to deepen perceptibly and to become permanent.

"Did you have any difficulty with Hooger and Birep?" he asked, after a thoughtful pause.

"Not the least, sire," responded the explorer.

"They readily saw, as the Princes had done, that resistance was out of the question."

For a few moments the King was silent, as if he had reached a full presentation of the case and was deliberating upon it.

"What ought to be done with them, Sabat?" he then asked, turning to his thin and weazened minister.

"They ought to be tried and executed within twenty-four hours," advised the Premier, "or at least executed."

"You didn't intend to give them a trial, did you, Sabat?"

"No, sire," answered the Premier, "it's enough that they've entered Your Majesty's dominions with arms in their hands, and have made war upon Your Majesty's subjects—offenses punished with death by all civilized nations."

"What fine men!" whispered the Princess Rubal. "What a gain for us if we could only attach them to our service, papa!"

"Peace, girl," returned the monarch, in a like

tone, "let us hear what Sabat has further to advise on the subject."

The further advice of Sabat, however, was limited to a single observation.

All he had to say was that the three men should be locked up over night and executed at an early hour of the morning.

"Only in this way can we take suitable action against this intrusion," he declared, "and prevent the Progressives from entering upon a renewed agitation that may cost Your Majesty the throne of the great Aryon!"

"So be it!" returned the King, with the air and manner of having set his face definitely against the invaders. "They must die, of course."

"Oh, papa—no, no!" protested the Princess Rubal. "We cannot afford to throw away such lives as these—never! Then there are the girl and the clergyman, who have not yet had a word to say in regard to their intrusion. Let us hear them both before we proceed to extremities."

"Very well—we'll hear them."

Mr. Haddon took a step or two forward, but King Polaria stopped him by a gesture.

" We'll hear the girl first," he declared, " and it's possible," he added with a smile, intended to put her at her ease, " that we shall not need to hear any one else."

## CHAPTER XXIII.

### *The Explanations of the Explorers—An Exciting Arrival.*

IT is doubtful if Alice Haddon had ever before looked as beautiful as she did at the moment of advancing a few steps nearer to the King of Polaria to enter upon her proposed explanations.

And this beauty was not merely a loveliness of person, in form, outline or color, but it was also and more particularly a radiance from within, a beauty of soul and mind, a gleam from her heart of the tender love and admiration she had already conceived for the daring explorer.

Then, too, she felt that the very lives of her loved ones might depend upon her power of setting forth the facts in the case clearly, and thus showing the innocence of the invaders of any very serious wrongdoing.

" It has been my misfortune, sire," she began, in

a voice as charming as her face, "to meet Prince Ardeb, and to be loved by him."

"Loved!" repeated the King, with a start.

"Admired and loved to such an extent, sire," continued the girl, "that he has begged me a hundred times during the last two weeks to accept his hand in marriage."

The King started again, as if he found it difficult to credit these declarations, but another keen glance into the sweet, pure face of Alice was enough to banish forever any theory or suggestion of her untruthfulness.

"Where did you make Prince Ardeb's acquaintance?" he asked.

Alice told him briefly, relating the facts already developed at length in this narrative.

"And how often have you seen him since that first meeting?"

The answer was promptly given.

"Did you know during any of these dealings that he was a Prince?"

"No, sire. He gave his name as Pirr Garvel, and his residence as 'over yonder hills to the northward.' I believed from the first, however, that his home was among the people residing at the Pole."

"Did you believe in our existence before you saw us?"

"Certainly, sire, as did Mr. Andree."

"And now to tell us of your rescue by Mr. Andree," suggested the monarch, with an air which revealed clearly enough that she was making a good impression upon him.

Alice told the story of her rescue accordingly, and it is almost needless to say that it would have been impossible for her to tell it without betraying that she had given her heart to the gallant explorer.

"And now a word as to who and what is your father," suggested the monarch, when he had looked as clearly into her relations with Andree, as into those of Prince Ardeb.

It can easily be imagined how simply but clearly she set forth the life and work of the good preacher, his lifelong interest in polar exploration; the unfortunate voyage which had plunged him into such dire distresses, and all else that seemed necessary to establish her father's footing upon its correct basis.

"Would you have accepted my son if you had known he is the Crown Prince of Polaria?" asked the King, interrupting her by a gesture, when her simple, filial testimony had told him, beyond all question, that Mr. Haddon was one of the noblest and least dangerous of men.

'No, sire.   I could not have accepted him under any circumstances whatever."

"Not even before you had met Herr Andree?"

"No, not even before that time," she responded, blushing to the very tips of her ears.

"And why couldn't you have accepted him?"

"For the simple reason that I did not love him."

"And now, Herr Andree," pursued the King, "let us hear what explanation you have to offer of this extraordinary visitation."

"Thanks, most gracious King," returned Andree, his clear, calm voice echoing throughout the apartment.   "From my youth I have been an earnest student of the world's history and the world's glories, thus being brought to a recognition of the first and (in some respects) the chiefest glory of our race, namely, the existence and work of the great mother nation, the Aryans, of whom Your Majesty is to-day the nearest and noblest representative."

From the sort of lethargy of surprise into which he had temporarily descended, King Polaris suddenly warmed into new life under the influence of these true and eloquent declarations.

"By my soul!" he ejaculated, drawing himself erect briskly and looking at Rubal with an approving and admiring air, "this is a mighty fine beginning!"

Turning anew to Andree, who had accompanied his concluding words with a profound inclination, the monarch said to him :

"You are aware, then, are you, Herr Andree, that the great primitive family of the Aryans once had their seat of empire at and near the North Pole?"

"I am not only aware of that fact, sir," replied the explorer, "but I deduced from it, years ago, that other and newer fact, namely, that there must

inevitably exist hereabouts a branch of the human
family descended in a direct line from that great
mother.   In other terms, sire, I figured out your
existence and that of your people, as a necessary
and irrefutable deduction from the known ; and I
knew ten years ago, as well as I know now, that I
should find you here, in case I could ever pass the
Polar Pack and reach latitude ninety."

"Capital!" commented the monarch, his features
brightening.   "You knew us before you saw us !
And is that the secret of your persistence in
seeking means and money to make this descent
upon us ?"

"The truth of the whole matter, sire," replied
Andree ; "I had not merely a conviction that I
should find such and such a state of things here,
but I had reasoned out the deduction that I must
surely find it, and thus secured a sort of foreknowledge of the facts awaiting my coming."

"I see that you are no common man, Herr Andree," commented the King, "and I dare say that
Herr Fraenckel and the doctor are well worthy of
their distinguished leader and companion.   Minis-

ter Sabat and I have evidently acted a little hastily in taking such severe measures against you, but, by way of excusing us, you should remember that we have lived for years under a sort of panic produced by the fear that the great nations of the earth would fall upon us and rend us in pieces as soon as they should get to know of our existence. Am I right or not, Herr Andree, in cherishing this apprehension ?"

"Your Majesty is not only wise in entertaining this fear," replied Andree, " but it would be a great mistake to ever let down the bars to the slightest extent or in any particular."

" I thank you, Herr Andree," said the monarch, with his most genial voice and kindly air, " and if you will excuse the haste with which we have acted, why we will overlook all that you and yours have done amiss since your arrival in Polaria, and nothing shall be left undone on our part to put our relations upon a most excellent footing !"

The explorers all hastened singly and in chorus to give expression to their thanks for these very gratifying declarations.

"Good !" commented the monarch, arising. " It is understood, Herr Andree, that you and your friends will remain my guests until further advices."

At this juncture another great tumult arose in front of the palace, calling every eye in that direction, and the captain of the guards again presented himself in great haste to his royal master.

" The princes are coming in their airships, both of them, Your Majesty," was his hurried announcement.

" How can that be?" asked the monarch.

"I cannot say for a certainty," admitted the officer, " but Hooger and Birep both think that the engineers and firemen merely made a pretense of getting away in order to get rid of the strangers."

" Be that as it may," said the king, " here they come," and in another minute the two princes— Ardeb and Volpan, otherwise Pirr Garvel and Swib Neerec—came hurrying into the monarch's presence, closely followed by Captain Stobeck.

## CHAPTER XXIV.

*The Explorers the Guests of King Polaris—Wrath*
*of the Princes.*

THE admission of Prince Ardeb and his companions to the reception-room of the palace was not
refused, the captain of the guards having received
a nod from his master.

"Ah, there you are!" was the greeting of the
King to his brother and son, in a dubious voice,
and with a still more dubious manner, as he looked
inquiringly from one to the other.

"Most Gracious Majesty," began the two Princes
in chorus, inclining their supple figures almost to
the floor ; but the monarch interrupted them with
a glance and gesture of extreme reprobation, de-
manding :

"Why are you here ?"

"May it please your Royal Majesty," replied
Ardeb, "we were so badly treated by these in-

vaders, that we feared for Your Majesty's life, and
hastened to follow them hither ———"

"You could have spared yourselves the trouble,"
interrupted the King, icily. "These 'invaders'
are not at all dangerous. Herr Andree is actuated
by a higher regard for our national glories than
you have ever shown, and it has been a rare pleasure for me to make his acquaintance, and that of
his worthy companions."

Prince Ardeb bowed his head, as one who re-
ceives a severe rebuke, but a deadly gleam of
hatred shot from his eyes in the direction of the
explorers.

"I hear from Miss Haddon," continued the King,
"that you made her acquaintance two weeks ago,
when she was eight or ten degrees south of the
place of your banishment. How do you explain
that fact, sir?"

"I was merely trying a new governor I had at-
tached to the balloon, sire," responded the Prince,
"and had a great deal of trouble and danger with
it, getting carried out of my course. And when, at
length, I encountered the wreck, I could do no less

than board it, to see if any persons were there in
need of assistance."

" Nevertheless, you gave the Haddons no assistance, so far as I have been able to discover," declared the King, sternly. " You left them to their
sufferings and privations—left them to perish, even,
as they would have gone to the bottom with the
wreck, if Herr Andree had not chanced to come to
the rescue."

" That was the girl's own fault, sire," protested
the Prince, bitterly.

" How her own fault?'

" Why, I offered to save her and her father,"
explained Ardeb, " if she would be sensible, and
promise to take my suit for her hand into consideration."

A stormy flash of anger passed over the face of
the monarch.

" And has it come to this, sir," he demanded, his
voice husky with anger, " that a prince descended
from Aryon the Great has fallen so low that he can
force his unwelcome attentions upon a lady?
Sinjib !"

The faithful servitor hastened to approach, signifying by a profound inclination that he was awaiting orders.

"Sinjib," said the King, "you will take Miss Haddon to the First Lady in Waiting and see that she is installed in the Blue Room."

Sinjib bowed understandingly.

"The missionary you will lodge in the room next to his daughter, the Red Parlor."

Again Sinjib inclined his tall figure attentively.

"And as to the Swedes," pursued the King, "we'll make them at home in my private ante-chamber, as I expect to have a great deal to say to Herr Andree. Place Tootil at their disposal, and see that they do not want for anything during their stay with us."

Turning away with a final inclination to execute these orders, Sinjib placed himself in touch with the explorer and his party, conducting them to their several quarters, and carefully repeating to those concerned all the orders he had received for their comfort.

"You may go to your quarters, Captain Stobeck," resumed the King, addressing that officer, "and await there our further pleasure."

Stobeck vanished accordingly, leaving the Princes alone with their monarch, with the exception of Rubal ; the captain of the guards, at a gesture from his master, having cleared the reception-room of all the intruders who had forced their way into it at the moment of the Prince's arrival.

" And now a serious word to you both," resumed the monarch, his glances alternating with marked severity from his son to his brother.

" In the presence of the Princess, sire ?" ventured Volpan, indicating Rubal by a gesture.

" Oh, yes, in the presence of the Princess," answered the King. " She is not only near to me, but she is honorable and honest—more than I can say for the rest of you—and I have no word to say to you or any one else that she may not hear."

The Princes inclined themselves profoundly, as if making up in outward show what they lacked in affection and reverence.

" You both know why I banished you to Mastodon Island," resumed the King, his glances again

flashing from one to the other. " It was because you
had been detected in a conspiracy to remove me
from the throne and replace me—as if either of you
possessed the stirrups for that sort of saddle !"

" Forgive us, sire!" implored Volpan.

" We beg anew for mercy!" said Prince Ardeb.

" And it's evident that you have not pleaded in
vain, or you would be looking through barred windows at this moment," declared the King stormily.
" As you are both well aware, I was ashamed to
let the nation know that I had a son and brother
capable of plotting against me, and so I gave out
that you had been banished for refusing to accept
the bride I had selected for you."

" I am willing to accept her now," returned
Ardeb.

" And I am wholly at Your Majesty's disposal,
begging again for forgiveness," said Volpan.

" Well, you can go home to your family,
brother," said the King, " but I warn you to never
again place yourself in the position of a conspirator
against my throne and people."

" I never will, sire," protested Volpan, seizing

the hand of the King and imprinting several kisses
upon it before permitting its withdrawal. " I will
endeavor henceforth to be the most loyal subject
Your Majesty possesses."

"Good-by, then, and good fortune attend you."

The remark was accompanied by an imperative
wave of the hand, and Volpan lost no time in obey-
ing it, taking his departure.

"As to you, my son," resumed the King, his
eyes luminous with gloom and sadness, "what can I
say to you?   What can I do to place our relations
upon a satisfactory footing, or even establish a
*modus vivendi ?*"

" Take me back to your heart and home, father,"
pleaded Ardeb, with a well-simulated gust of re-
pentance.   " Restore me to the footing I have for-
feited and I will never again be found wanting in
affection and honor."

"One word first," said the King.   " You have
seen that these new-comers are my guests?"

The Prince bowed, wondering to what this remark would lead.

" And as such they are not to be molested by you,

Ardeb," continued the monarch. " Do you understand that Miss Haddon and Herr Andree are
lovers, actual or avowed ?"

The Prince assented, not caring to trust his voice
to speak.

"You can see at a glance, therefore," continued
the King, "that you must refrain from saying
another word to that girl about love or marriage."

"I will refrain accordingly," promised Ardeb,
"and turn my aspirations in some new channel."

"And now as to your coming back here," said
the monarch. "I cannot say to-day how soon I
I will restore you to favor, but I am willing to open
the way for you. Your cousin, the Princess
Volpie, is not likely to find a suitable match for a
long time to come unless you marry her, and that
outcome is one which has been receiving our favorable consideration for a number of weeks past.
What do you think of it ?"

"I will obey Your Majesty in that respect as in
every other," was the Prince's answer.

"Very well, Ardeb," declared the monarch, adding : "You may constitute yourself the guest of

your uncle for the present, and see if a union between you and the Princess Volpie is possible or
desirable."

"Many thanks, sire," responded the Prince,
averting his face to conceal the expression of dis-
appointment which passed over it. "Then I am
not to remain here at present?"

"No, not until after Herr Andree and his friends
have left me. Good-by for the present."

The Prince had no sooner gone, with ill-dis-
sembled wrath and mortification, than Rubal turned
anew to the monarch, caressing him:

"I like those Swedes and that girl," she declared,
"and have no doubt we shall enjoy their visit
greatly."

"And it may be that something better than mere
recreation and enjoyment will come of it," suggested the monarch. "If I can attach all of them
to us sufficiently for them to remain here, we shall
certainly be the gainers."

"And may I accompany you, papa, when you
take Mr. Haddon and Herr Andree to see the
city?"

The monarch assented.

"And—and, is it too much to ask that the doctor—Mr. Strindberg—may come with us, papa?" asked Rubal, hiding her face in the royal bosom.

"Oh, that's how the land lays, is it?" returned the King, with a jovial air, caressing her. "Well, well, puss! Your Dr. Strindberg is welcome to be of the party."

## CHAPTER XXV.

*The Golden City of the Pole—The Explorers Enjoy the Royal Favor.*

SEATED in a large four-wheeled automobile, the King and his guests were whirled rapidly through the parks and boulevards of the polar capital.

"And have you no horses, sire?" asked Andree, after a silence of wonder and admiration, which had lasted a number of minutes.

"None, Mr. Andree," was the monarch's answer. "It has been thousands of years since one was seen in Polaria."

"Why is that, sire? Is the climate fatal to them?"

"Oh, no; but we had no use for them. With balloons for the skies and automobiles for the earth, very few would be willing to be bothered with the care of horses."

"And you have no cows, I see."

"No, for the reason that we have no use for them," explained the King. "We have a cow-plant which gives a far better milk than the animal, at no perceptible cost or trouble, and hence our people could not possibly be brought to the slavery of waiting upon such creatures."

"Well, not having cows, the Polarians do not have beef or slanghter-houses ?'

"Nothing of the kind," agreed the monarch, smiling. "We have plants which supply us with all the life-giving elements supposed to reside in meat and game, and I doubt if there is a man in my kingdom so—so made as to be capable of kill-ing a lamb, calf or chicken."

"You do not have dogs, even ?"

"No, for the reason that dogs would simply be a burden and an affliction. As a rule, those who kept dogs, in the old days, were found to lavish upon them the regards due to humanity, and hence, one of my ancestors issued a decree which wiped out the canine race, altogether."

Another silence succeeded, the attention of the

explorers being given to the beauties of a vast public garden into which the motor had turned.

" And is the tropical warmth we experience here,
sire," resumed Andree, "all derived from the internal heat of the earth ?"

" Not all of it ; but the larger share of it," answered the monarch. " You shall see our borings
and tubings ; they are on a scale that will surprise
you. Polaris the First was the original discoverer
of the fact that the internal fires of our globe are
nearer to us at the Pole than elsewhere, on account
of the depression produced there by the revolution
of the earth upon its axis when it was in a molten
and fluid condition. And having made that discovery, Polaris the First set about turning it to
account, entering upon these vast tappings of the
internal reservoirs which we have kept up ever
since."

It was with speechless amazement that the visitors surveyed the forests and oceans of flowers
around them, including vines and flowering shrubs,
most of them of a size and species wholly unknown
to them until that moment.

" And how about the water necessary for all these growths?" demanded Andree.

"Oh, we get it up by millions of gallons from the lakes and ponds beneath us," replied the King, " and it comes to us in every desired state, from icy cold to boiling."

" But what are all these boxes and globes I see scattered throughout the city?" pursued the explorer.

" They are the storage boxes of our heat, which is a mixture of electricity and terrestrial magnetism, not to speak of a number of new elements associated therewith, and for the exact nature of which I must refer you to the Royal Electrician," responded the King. " It is enough to say at present that we have the heating of our city and kingdom under perfect control, and that the weather we manufacture for ourselves here the year around is as fine an article as you will find in the most favored tropics!"

" I see your houses are all detached, each of them occupying an acre or more, with the exception of the public buildings," observed Fraenckel, who had naturally been associated with his comrades in this survey of the city.

"Yes, and there is a good reason for that fact," explained King Polaris. "The families who live in these houses are obliged to raise their own food upon the ground around them."

"I see, too, that you have very few buildings exceeding three stories."

"Very few, sir."

"It seems to me, too, that there is nothing going on here—no commerce, no hurry and worry ; none of those things which are called the bustle of business and the glory of civilization," observed Dr. Strindberg.

"We have very few of the aspects of London or New York, I must confess," returned the King, his smile deepening.

"You don't even have any money?" said Alice.

"No ; for the reason that we have no use for it," explained King Polaris. "But we have something you will never see in any other part of the world, and that is a mountain of gold."

The explorers echoed the phrase in astonishment.

"In good truth, we care no more here for gold than we do for silver or copper, except so far as it has its useful qualities in excess of other metals," pursued the royal host, with the air of enjoying the surprise of his guests at all they saw around them. "I will show you the mountain later, as also a vein leading from it for hundreds of miles across our country."

"And how few people there are stirring at this moment!" exclaimed Andree, looking around upon two or three automobiles in sight, and a dozen pedestrians.

"And most of these seem to be very old men," supplemented Fraenckel.

"And such they are," said the King. "We have hosts of people in our midst, men and women, who have entered their third century. How those results are reached, I will tell you later in the leisure of my library. Do you find the air here in any way oppressive?"

"No, sire, only exhilarating and exciting," replied Andree.

"Perhaps some of you have had enough of it for

to-day," suggested the monarch, with a glance into the faces around him.  " I intended this first visit to be a short one, but we will repeat it to-morrow and every day for a week to come, and by that time you will know all about us, and be so acclimated that you can do as we do."

He made a gesture to his motorman, and in a few minutes the royal host and his guests were again at the palace.

## CHAPTER XXVI.

*Singular Fates and Fortunes Dawning upon the
Explorers—Alice and Andree.*

IT was a month later.

During this interval the explorers and the Haddons had remained the guests of the monarch, rid-
ing with him several hours daily, and taking note of
all the wonders and curiosities the Golden City of
the Pole had to offer.

And at the end of this time, it is needless to say,
the visitors had reached the conclusion that a more
singular civilization than that of Polaria has never
been seen upon our planet.

To begin  with, the Polarians are strict vegeta-
rians, finding in the fruits and vegetables they raise
in their gardens—each household cultivating on its
own account—all the nourishment they require.

To fruits and vegetables they have learned to
add electricity, terrestrial magnetism, and the un-

dulations of the cosmic ether, in such proportions and under such conditions as to double the average life of man, as compared with that of the inhabitants of any other country of the globe.

In his room at the royal palace sat the Rev. Mr. Haddon, in the midst of the vast array of books and manuscripts the monarch had placed at his disposal, and with which he had been busy since an early hour of the morning.

" Surely, it is good to be the guest of such a king as Polaris XLVII," he exclaimed, his face glowing with the zeal of a theologian and antiquarian. " I would like nothing better than to pass the balance of my days precisely as I have passed the last month."

A gentle knock at the entrance caught his hearing and a pleasant voice demanded : " May I come in, papa?"

"Of course, you may, my dear child," returned the father, springing up and advancing a chair for her use. " I shall be glad to have the recreation your presence will give me."

Alice sat down near him, looking bright and conented, so happy and bewitching that he could not refrain from leaning over and pressing a kiss upon her forehead with all a father's pride and tenderness.

"And where have you been all this long day, daughter?" he resumed, returning to his seat, but without picking up the great folio which had monopolized his attention during several hours.

"With Mr. Andree, as usual, papa," was the answer. "We have been to see again the great ocean of lava which has poured from the Central Crater, and which will remain a storehouse of heat for the Golden City during many a long year to come."

"Have you made any new friends to-day?"

"Scores of them, including the most distinguished ladies of the kingdom. Many of them," she added, "have expressed the hope that I will see my way to remaining here a few years, if not forever. And as to Andree, you should see how the Polarians throng around him whenever he becomes visible. Excepting the King, he is already the most popular man in Polaria."

"The speeches he has delivered against reveal-

ing the existence of Polaria to the outer world have
certainly made an excellent impression," returned
the clergyman. "The King himself was speaking
to me about them at the dinner table. I was just
wishing you would drop in upon me, as I am full
to overflowing of the revelations of these wonderful volumes."

"And of the equally wonderful daily life of these
people, I presume," said Alice, with a sigh of intense interest. "How odd that there should be no
prisons here, no hospitals, no jails, no poor-houses,
and none of those other institutions we regard as
the great evidences and necessities of our civilization!"

"And how singular that there should be no doc-
tors or lawyers, no courts or judges, no poor persons and no wealthy ones, no paupers and no mil-
lionaires, no criminals and no beggars!"

"And is it not equally strange that there should
be no butchers or grocers, no employers or em-
ployees, no railroads and no telegraph, no ships and
no commerce, none of that competition which is

worrying all the other nations of the world out of existence ?"

" And just think, papa, how odd it is that the Polarians should have ten or a dozen different kinds of cloth plants, or plants whose leaves furnish ready made all the textures required for the clothes of the people, both ladies and gentlemen ; as also all the sheets and blankets required for bedding ?"

" Yes, that is certainly a curious provision of nature," responded the father, " since it renders unnecessary wool and cotton and all those other fabrics we are in the habit of using. But all this is as nothing to the history of these Polarians, which I have been tracing to-day through more than twenty thousand years."

" Do you find that they are really descended from the Aryans ?"

" I do, Alice ; and I find that they have lived in and around the Pole more centuries than are allowed for the existence of the earth by our narrow-minded teachers. That man first appeared upon the earth at the North Pole, as we have recently seen stated, I have no doubt whatever. But these are studies, my dear child, you must take up with me. I've never passed such a joyous month in my life as I have passed in this palace."

" Nor have I, papa !" returned Alice, a vivid flush invading cheeks and forehead. " I wouldn't have believed that love is such a great glory and gladness, if I had not experienced the fact in my own heart and life !"

" Then you are getting on all right with Mr. Andree, are you, daughter ?"

" As nicely as can be."

" Has he asked you to marry him ?"

" Just a few minutes ago, papa," replied Alice, " and I told him my heart has been his since that awful hour when he met us on that drifting wreck. Needless to add, papa, that I count upon your consent and approval when he speaks to you about this matter."

" You will not count upon me in vain, my dear child," declared the clergyman, caressing her. " I could not love Mr. Andree more if he were my own son, nor is there a man on earth for whom I have greater respect."

A firm tread resounded in the corridors at this moment, and the explorer made his appearance in the best of health and spirits. The greetings he exchanged with the clergyman were unusually full of feeling.

"I suppose Alice has told you, Mr. Haddon, what has passed between us," he demanded.

"She has, my dear boy," was the answer, "and it is needless to say how delighted I am that you have come to an understanding."

"I called at the King's library to acquaint him with the new position of our affairs," pursued Andree, his arm stealing around the shapely waist of his betrothed, "but Sabat was discussing some important matter with him and he asked me to return in fifteen or twenty minutes."

"Sit down," invited Mr. Haddon, "and we'll discuss the question of our return to America. Not that anything pressing is calling us back, or that I am tired of Polaria—to the contrary—but there is quite a tribe of us, and I wish to avoid wearing out our welcome."

"Oh, we can't return yet, papa," said Andree.

"The King wouldn't hear of such a thing, and I have not yet really begun to investigate the thousand and one problems hurled at me by the career and situation of this strange people. Finding ourselves in such an excellent position for the study of Polaria and its inhabitants, past and present, we must certainly remain here awhile longer ——"

An exciting cry of alarm rang through the corridor at this instant, from the direction of the King's apartments, followed by the hurried trampling of feet.

"Quick, Sinjib! Get Dr. Erlon here!" the King was heard calling.

"Ah! something is wrong!" exclaimed the explorer, starting for the King's apartments. "Follow me, please."

## CHAPTER XXVII.

*A New Order of Events—The Explorer Attains
to the Highest Honors*

IN one of the fine rooms of her suite in the royal
palace sat the Princess Rubal, with a face so radiant that the least impressionable observer would
have been obliged to pronounce it beautiful—it was
a mirror of such womanly tenderness, such an over-
flow of the heart, such a natural and spontaneous
evolution of the master passion.

"Oh I love him !" escaped her as she clasped
her hands, a look of dreamy gladness appearing in
her eyes. "And I am sure that he loves me as
fondly as I love him. This dear and charming
Doctor Strindberg !"

"Then why don't he say so?" demanded her
maid.

Rubal started as if from a trance.

"Did I speak, Eifet?" she inquired,

"Speak, Your Royal Highness?" returned Eifet,
"I should say so! You ought to have seen yourself in a mirror!"

"Why, what was I doing?"

"You were just going to and fro like a lion in
its cage, and "——

"Just thinking aloud, I suppose?" interrupted
Rubal, with a flush of mingled surprise and mortification. "Fortunately no indiscreet eyes were
upon me. Since you have surprised my secret,
however, or it has surprised you—no matter about
defining just how the truth has leaked out—tell
me, dear, what you think of the young doctor?"

"Oh, I think he's grand," replied Eifet. "Just
grand! for you, I mean!"

"And why for me, rather than anybody else?"

"Well, because Your Royal Highness is like
him," explained the maid. "You are like him and
can hold your own with him. You know all about
mutations, quadrants, hexameters and other things
that would worry me to death if I had to carry
them around with me, but you just seem to enjoy

the learning and big words that flow from the lips of the doctor!"

"Well, I do—that's a fact," admitted the Princess. "But you were asking me, in substance, why the doctor hadn't proposed to me? He's afraid of papa—he's afraid of me! He may fear that he has no chance of being accepted by either of us—either by the Princess or monarch!"

"Or he may have no home to offer you," suggested Eifet.

"Then he can leave me just where I am and I will offer him a share of mine," declared Rubal. "The essential—but here he comes! You may leave me for awhile, Eifet, after showing him in."

The meeting of the young couple was not without some constraint on both sides, but it was nevertheless very pleasant to both, if their expectant manner could be trusted.

"I was wishing you'd come," said Rubal, accepting the bright flowers he handed her and beginning at once to tear them in pieces. "Where have you been all the morning?"

"Oh, I have been to the Silver Grotto again, taking a magnetic bath," replied Strindberg. " Did Your Royal Highness miss me ?"

" Yes, my ' Royal Highness' was a good deal fretted by your prolonged absence. Are you get-ting tired of Polaria ?"

" As if I could be so long as Your Royal High-ness is in it."

" Are you having a good time here, Dr. Strind-berg ?"

" Oh, the finest any man ever had anywhere !"

" Would you like to stay here forever ?"

" I would indeed—if I could be near you !"

"Why don't you remain, then ?"

" Why, I—I—that is, Your Royal High-ness —— "

" I beg to suppress ' Your Royal Highness,' Dr. Strindberg," declared the girl stormily. " Call me Rubal, since that is my name !"

"Dare I take such liberties, Your—Rubal ?"

" I don't know why you shouldn't, since papa takes such liberties with me."

" Rubal it shall be, then, since you are so gra-cious to me."

"And since you are so much in love with Po-laria," pursued the girl, tearing her handful of flowers in pieces and throwing them in his face, "Why don't you stay here always?"

"Oh, if I might speak of the all-absorbing pas-sion——"

"Well, why don't you speak of it? You have a tongue, haven't you?"

"But you, the only daughter of a king, and I, a poor explorer, without friends or fortune——"

"There you are again in the same old banalities! As if an acre of ground isn't all the fortune one needs in Polaria!"

"May I dare hope, then——"

He hesitated, looking startled, as if afraid his love for her had made him too bold.

"Yes, you may hope—if you will talk fast," re-turned Rubal, hiding her glowing face under his chin. "I am 'Your Royal Highness,' it is true, but I am also a woman, with a woman's heart, and —and I have loved you ever since you entered this palace!"

We need not linger upon the response of the

young explorer to these gracious and considerate admissions. That his reply was adequate and acceptable may be taken for granted.

"And now let us go and see papa about this thing," proposed Rubal, passing a brush over the hair he had ruffled. " I want to be sure of my happiness."

Arm in arm, their faces a revelation, they sauntered into the presence of King Polaris, who had just turned away from the contemplation of some state document his Premier had placed before him.

" What have we here ?" he ejaculated, a smile of welcome breaking over his face as he looked from one to the other.

"A son and a daughter, papa," avowed Rubal, as both knelt at his feet. " You have never yet refused your little girl anything reasonable, papa——"

" And do you think it reasonable, my dear child, to take this stranger into our family ?" returned the monarch, passing his hand caressingly over her head.

"Oh, it's more than reasonable, papa—it is absolutely necessary."

"For you, perhaps; but what has he to say about it?" asked the King. "I don't see as he is very talkative."

"Because, sire, I am confounded by the great joy which has come so unexpectedly to me," declared Strindberg, seizing the King's hand and showering kisses upon it. "If I am dumb, it's because language is powerless to tell Your Majesty how fondly I love this dear girl, how warmly I worship her and admire her, and how ready I am to die for either or both of you——"

"It's all right, my son," said the monarch, his face illuminated by a smile of the rarest kindness. "You shall have her, doctor, with my fondest blessing. I have noticed what tender ties exist between you and Herr Andree, and I hail these proceedings as a first step towards keeping your distinguished associate permanently with us."

He waved the couple to chairs near him, kissing Rubal and embracing the doctor, and proceeded:

"Here comes Sabat.  You may remain to hear what he has to say to me."

The Premier was shown into the room in accordance with usage and standing orders, but he came to a halt just within the entrance, looking at the monarch and at the young couple as if he had found in their faces or attitudes a surprising and painful revelation.

"Ah, perhaps I have come at an inopportune moment," he said, bowing to the Princess and inclining himself to the monarch.  "If so——"

His voice ceased suddenly, and he fell in a heap to the floor.

It was then that the King uttered the cry of alarm which had reached the hearing of Andree and the Haddons in the adjacent apartment, and called them in that direction.

When they arrived they found that Sinjib and others had raised the Premier and placed him upon a sofa, but a single glance told them that life had departed.

A few moments were given to the shock natural

to such an event, and then the King turned to Andree, taking him by the hand.

" This occurence has long been foreseen and expected," he said, " and it couldn't have come at a more timely moment.   I invite you, Herr Andree, to become Sabat's successor !"

## CHAPTER XXVIII.

### The Princess and Volpie—Another Conspiracy with a Menace for Andree.

IN the residence of Prince Volpan, which was imposing and extensive enough to be deemed a palace, the Prince was pacing nervously to-and-fro, in a state of unwonted excitement.

"What worries you so, papa?" demanded the Princess Volpie, his only daughter, arriving suddenly from her own apartments.

She drew his arm within her own with a very pretty assumption of authority, and began walking to-and-fro with him, awaiting his answer.

She was not at all pretty, not even having regular features, but she was plump and well-rounded, and had received attention enough from governesses and others to possess a fair degree of culture, gracefulness and polish.

" I want you to look at the bright side of things,

papa, from this hour onward," resumed the girl, patting the arm she had taken. "The truth is, papa, I have excellent news for you if you are ready to hear it."

"Excellent news," he repeated with a dubious countenance, conducting her to a sofa and seating her upon it, then placing himself beside her. "You are jesting surely?"

"Not at all, papa."

"Then tell me what your good news is."

"Why, cousin and I have had many long conversations since his return from Mastodon Island, and the result is that we have reached the conclusion to unite our fates and fortunes."

The Prince looked the Princess over a few moments in silence.

"I do not wonder your cousin is drawn to you," he then said, "for you are a girl that cannot be matched in ten thousand. But what you can see in Ardeb to attract you surpasses my comprehension."

"Well, he's neither good nor handsome," affirmed the Princess, "but he's resolute and energetic, and I have no doubt he will be a wise king when he comes to the throne of his father."

She placed her rosy lips close to the ear of Volpan and added :

" Which event may come far sooner than it is expected."

" Ah, has Ardeb said as much as that to you ?"

" He has, papa—in confidence. The fact is, that Polaris XLVII. is the oldest monarch who has reigned in Polaria for several centuries."

" Yes, he's old," admitted Volpan, " but he's as tough as he's old, and I don't see just yet how his days are to be shortened. If the Prince has really decided to take some definite action in the premises —but here he comes."

It was with a very gloomy countenance that the Prince sauntered into the presence of the father and daughter.

" Why, Ardeb, cousin, what can ail you ?" cried Volpie, springing to her feet and hastening to meet him.

" Haven't you told her the news, Uncle ?" de-

manded the newcomer, halting abruptly and looking from one to the other.

"Not yet, nephew.  I was just coming to that as
you entered."

"Then she doesn't know what has happened at
the palace ?"

"Nothing whatever."

It was now Volpie's turn to be alarmed and
anxious.

"Speak !" she cried, looking from her betrothed
to her father.  "What is it that's wrong at the
palace ?"

"Everything," replied Ardeb.  "To begin with,
Sabat has dropped dead "——

"Good ! the hideous old meddler and critic, not
to say cynic.  But isn't his death our gain?  Isn't
there a chance for papa to be taken into his
brother's counsel ?  May he not even be appointed
to Sabat's place ?"

"One would suppose so, certainly," commented
Volpan, "since I am the only brother he has, and
am the representative of the only large party we

have ever had in Polaria, but the King did not so
much as think of me for a moment."

"No? Then it may be that he will give the
place to Ardeb "——

"Don't!" pleaded the Prince, interrupting his
betrothed with an air of wrath and disgust.  "The
son is of as little account as the uncle, and neither
can be compared for a moment with that Swede.
In a word, Andree is now Premier of Polaria !"

"Impossible !"

"It's only too true," assured Ardeb, with sullen
wrathfulness.  "The death of Sabat was no sooner
known to the King than he hastened to find the
Swede and offer the place to him."

"But how dare he appoint a foreigner to the
first post in the kingdom ?"

"Oh, the fact that the man's a Swede cuts no
figure in the premises.  The truth is, Andree has
made a number of speeches during the week which
have rendered him popular with all parties."

"Is this so, papa ?"

"Of course it is," assured Volpan.  "He has
convinced my old party, or at least the best men in

it—the so-called Liberal party, whose watchword was the opening of Polaria to the world—that such a movement would be inevitably a suicide, leading to our destruction as a people and government. As to the Conservatives, it's needless to say that they are all with the Swede—every one of them— and that he could not show himself to them to-night without being hailed as a veritable deliverer."

A long silence followed this exposition of the situation.

"And now you see where we are, Volpie," resumed her father. "You can indeed marry your cousin if you see fit, but both he and I are little better than beggars!"

"Then what's to be done?" asked the girl, with a change of color.

"Of course you two will marry?" queried Volpan.

"Most assuredly," answered Volpie; "if we only have the clothes we stand in."

"I've no objection to that, but it will be necessary for us to unite upon some course of action looking to the betterment of our situation.   What shall it be?"

"Suppose you give us your advice, uncle," suggested Ardeb.

"Well, my advice can be put into a nutshell," declared Volpan, with an energy born of desperation and anger.  "We had better get out of Polaria, since no proper place for us can be found in it."

"How get out, uncle?"

"Go aboard of The Flyer and take our flight to New York, the Western world's great centre."

"And what can we do there?"

"Place in the hands of the wealthiest men in New York a sample of our golden mountain and tell them we have in sight fifty million tons of it. The rest can be left to them."

"You mean they will prevail upon the Government of the United States to seize and hold Polaria?"

"Undoubtedly; and we shall accumulate by our royalties such a fortune as no man has ever seen," declared Volpan, his visage inflamed with greed and his eyes gleaming savagely. "Instead of starving here and being nobodies, we can revel in all those luxuries and enjoyments to which wealth is the key."

Volpie flushed as if fascinated by the picture her father had presented.

"Let's do it," she proposed, turning to Ardeb. "Let's leave Polaria this very night. Shall we, papa?"

"We will, if Ardeb says so!"

"Well, I do say so," declared the Prince emphatically. "I'll have everything in readiness by the time the palace is wrapped in slumber."

"But what have we to do with the palace?" asked Volpie.

"Only this," returned the Prince, "that I cannot think of leaving Polaria without paying a final visit to Herr Andree."

"Will you endeavor to get square with him for the annoyance he has caused you?" asked Volpan.

"That's just the point I have in view, uncle," replied Ardeb. "But you and Volpie are not called upon to share the risks of this visit with me. You can go direct to The Flyer and see that the boys get up steam in readiness to start at a moment's notice."

A little discussion enabled the trio to settle all the details of their proposed departure, and it was with a keen impatience that they awaited the hour of action.

## CHAPTER XXIX.

### *Prince Ardeb Busy.*

NIGHT had come again, but night in Polaria at that season of the year was hardly worthy of the name, the sun remaining only a short time below the horizon, and then resuming its sway as brightly as ever.

It was the hour usually devoted to sleep, however, and Ardeb started for the royal palace with the calm expectation and absolute probability of finding his intended victim wrapped in slumber.

"You have the key to the room the explorer is occupying?" questioned Volpan, as they were separating at the entrance of the latter's residence.

"Yes, I have it."

"Well, be as wary as possible, nephew," enjoined Dolpan, "and take good care not to make a failure of your scheme or to get into any trouble with it."

"Oh, I will be wary," assured the Prince, stow-

ing away upon his person one of those deadly
poisons only Polaria could have furnished. "If I
can gain admittance—but, of course, I shall allow
no 'ifs' to come between me and the execution of
my purpose."

"In the mean time Volpie and I will take possession of The Flyer," said Volpan, "and have
everything in readiness to leave at an instant's
warning."

With a nod of acquiescence, Ardeb stole away
quietly in the direction of the palace, while the
father and daughter hastened to finish their preparations.

If anything had been wanting to confirm Prince
Ardeb in the sinister resolution he had formed he
would have found it in the little notice that was
taken of him as he passed along the streets, and in
the general rejoicings that everywhere met his eye
over the nomination of Andree to the post of Prime
Minister.

"And to think that the cursed Swede has been
here only a month!" was the bitter comment of
the monarch's son, as he turned into one of the

most retired streets of the capital, to avoid a great
illumination which was presented in one of the
principal public squares. "Surely, fortune is as
certainly with him as misfortune is with me!"

Reaching the palace, he boldly entered the presence of the monarch, with the avowed object of
having come to congratulate him upon having
found such a worthy successor to Sabat.

"Really, my son?" returned Polaris, half incredu-
lously. "I was afraid you might be offended.
Perhaps I ought to have told you beforehand my
motives."

"Oh, no explanations are necessary, sire," returned Ardeb, dropping into the chair to which
the King had invited him by a gesture.

"Nevertheless, I ought to remind you, Ardeb,"
resumed the monarch, "that the situation of Polaria was never so ticklish as at this moment. If
any one should take it into his head to seize my
brother's torpedo-balloon or The Flyer and make
his escape to England or America, we should soon
have pouring in upon us a horde of gold-seekers

and robbers a thousand times worse than the Goths
and Vandals."

The Prince looked at his father sharply, reflect-
ing that he had long cherished this very species of
treachery, and that he had decided to carry it into
execution within the next two or three hours. He
reflected further that this treachery was no new
thought for him, he having been on his way to the
United States at the moment he encountered the
floating wreck, upon which he had made the
acquaintance of the Haddons.

"Yes, things will soon be in a bad way here if
the great powers got hold of us," he responded,
"but why should they, if we are careful?"

He talked in this way a number of minutes, play-
ing the hypocrite in a masterly fashion, but at
length arose to take his leave, making a pretence
of passing out of the palace.

Instead of taking this course, however, he concealed himself in one of the inner rooms of the
royal suite, which he knew had long been used as
a store-room, and here he watched and waited for
the hour of action.

And what a long and tiresome waiting succeeded will readily be imagined.

The explorers and the Haddons not only had a thousand pleasant hopes and ideas to exchange, under the new order of events, but the monarch himself was the victim of a restlessness he had never before experienced, so that he kept coming and going for hours, passing in and out of the rooms of his guests, not to speak of repeated visits to those of Andree and his daughter.

But at last all became still throughout the palace, its occupants having all retired for their wonted slumbers, and the intruder hastened to leave his concealment, taking his way to the apartment of Andree.

To his surprise and annoyance, the explorer was not there, and the Prince began a still hunt for him, which hunt soon brought him to the door of the room which had been assigned Alice Haddon.

At realizing that fact, the intruder halted abruptly. His one thought was still the slaying of Andree, but an irresistible temptation came over him to take a farewell look at the object of his passion, and he pushed open the door and entered.

She lay there, clearly revealed by the light, in the soundest of slumbers. As he looked, what a tumult invaded his soul! What a renewal of his passion came over him!

"Ah, if I could take her with me!" was the thought that flashed over him. "That would be a blow worse than death to the Swede—and a better vengeance and triumph for me than murder!"

To think was to act.

Stealing nearer, he produced a subtle poison, in the nature of chloroform, and held it to the nostrils of the fair sleeper a few moments, with the result that she passed from sleep to unconsciousness.

Fortunately, she was fully attired, sleep having surprised her while she was thinking over the exciting events of the day, and the intruder hastened to pass his stout arm around her, and lift her from the bed, taking a noiseless but hurried departure.

Once clear of the palace, all the wild jubilance of his soul found vent in a torrent of verbal rejoicings.

Just how he would get rid of his uncle and cousin, he did not yet see clearly, but leaving his helpless captive somewhere in the background, he could tell his relatives a good story, and so get rid of them.

Arriving at the scene of his proposed departure, Prince Ardeb found the crew of the airship awaiting him, but all that remained of The Flyer was a heap of unsightly ruins.

" What has happened?" he inquired, halting.

" The King has caused every airship in the country to be destroyed," was the answer.

" Ah! that's why he was so busy after I left him !"

" Exactly."

" He must have had his suspicions !"

A moment, still holding Alice Haddon in his arms, the Prince stood as if turned to stone.

His route cut off, his means of escape taken away from him, what remained ?

" And what of my uncle and cousin?" he de-manded.

" They were here, waiting for you," replied the

engineer of the demolished craft, "but they have gone back to their palace, telling me to send you there as soon as possible."

An alarm arose behind the Prince at this instant, and was succeeded by hasty footsteps, which rapidly became louder.

"Ah! the Swede!" he cried, the picture of consternation.

Behind Andree came Mr. Haddon, Sinjib and others.

One glance at them was enough to tell Prince Ardeb that he could not make his escape, unless he instantly dismissed all idea of taking Alice with him.

"So be it!" he ejaculated. "Better luck next time!"

Depositing the unconscious girl upon the ground, he turned and disappeared in silence.

## CHAPTER XXX.

*A Sudden Turn of Affairs—The Polarians Same as Other Men.*

Arriving at his uncle's, Prince Ardeb was met by his cousin, whose beautiful but wicked face was aglow with joy.

"Your father has had a chill," she reported, "and Dr. Deegri says his situation is dangerous."

"No wonder," returned Ardeb, his eyes gleaming. "He has been very busy to-night—very busy and excited. But ——"

His gaze suddenly grew intense, as if this sudden illness had appeared to him a just cause of suspicion.

"No, we haven't given him anything," declared the Princess, reading the unspoken inquiry. "He has just made himself ill by worry and overwork."

"But surely you are keeping something from me!"

" Only that Dr. Deegri says your father is a very sick man ! In fact, he cannot live !"

" Then my place is beside him !"

" True ! Did our messengers find you and give you a hint of this ?"

" No ; for the reason that I have been busy with my schemes against the Swede !"

" We were told a moment ago you had carried off Alice Haddon !"

" A mistake !" protested Ardeb. " I'll explain later how the report arose."

" In any case, come ! The sooner you are with your father the better. Ah, here is papa !"

An automobile was in waiting, and the three conspirators were soon on their way to the palace of the King.

" Not finding you, papa and I have done what we could without you," resumed Volpie, taking the hand of her betrothed. " Are you ready to make a good fight for the throne of your ancestors ?"

How the eyes of Prince Ardeb brightened at the suggestion !

" Depend upon me!" was his answer.

" Well, papa has already secured possession of Fort Polaris and the Arsenal for you, so that your cause is half won," pursued Volpie, " and he has received ample assurances that the chiefs of the army and navy will sustain you."

Nothing more was said until the conspirators had reached the royal palace, where they found the bodyguard of the household under arms.

" My father?" demanded Ardeb, with a face and manner suited to the occasion, as the officer in command of the guard inclined himself profoundly before him.

" He's very low, Prince!"

" Has he inquired for me ?"

" Constantly. The name of Your Royal Highness is on his lips at every moment! He has wondered and worried at your absence!"

The conspirators stole into the palace in silence, an immense crowd regarding them with breathless excitement and sorrow, not to say anxiety. They were met in the ante-chamber by Dr. Deegri himself, whose air and manner showed that his thoughts were with the rising sun, rather than with that which was setting so abruptly forever.

"Am I too late?" cried Ardeb, realizing the significance of the doctor's profound inclination.

"Too late, Your Royal Majesty," replied the wily courtier. "Your royal father—— "

He was interrupted by deafening shouts in the streets and within the palace.

"The King is dead! Long live the King!" was the burden of the cries arising from thousands of throats, and in less than a minute these cries were echoing throughout the whole city.

With the usual fickleness of court officials, no matter what their country or clime, the great majority of the Polarian magnates precipitated themselves towards the royal palace, every man of them determined to be the first to manifest his allegiance to the new monarch.

Needless to linger upon the events that succeeded. In a few minutes the body of the late King was in the hands of the undertakers, and Prince Ardeb, assuming the title of Ardeb the Second, was seated in state upon the throne he had so long coveted, and all the celebrities of the kingdom were pouring into his ears that flattery which is ever the food of monarchs.

## CHAPTER XXXI.

*A Wild Tragedy of the Northland—Conclusion.*

By the time Andree and the Rev. Mr. Haddon had recalled Alice to her senses, an automobile was beside them, Andree having left orders for it to follow them.

A few rapid sentences told his betrothed how she had been abducted by the Prince, and with what intent, and she dismissed the whole episode as one dismisses a disagreeable dream on awakening.

"Things are in a bad way at the palace," said Mr. Haddon, after expressing his joy at his daughter's recovery. "The King has been suddenly stricken with an illness which threatens his life, and the whole household is in a state of intense excitement. It was owing to this event that we so quickly discovered your absence."

He heaved a profound sigh, adding :

"In a word, my dear child, the King is dead, or dying, and our footing in Polaria has become at once precarious and menacing."

Ere another word could be exchanged, the Princess Rubal arrived in an automobile, accompanied by Dr. Strindberg and Fraenckel.

She was in tears and tremulous with a grief and agitation she could neither conceal nor master.

"Listen," said the doctor, raising his hand and looking back in the direction from which he had come.

All complied.

"You see?" he returned. "Ardeb is now King of Polaria, and our very lives are in the balance! The Princess Rubal, despite her great sorrow, was the first to realize our peril, and to decide that flight is our only resource. More, she has cast her fortune with ours, and will go with us!"

All eyes turned upon the Princess, as if to seek verification of the statement.

"It is true," she said brokenly. "The will of my uncle and cousin is now supreme in Polaria, and I have no desire to remain here another moment !"

"And Andree?" demanded Alice Haddon, her hand stealing into that of her betrothed.

" My career as a favorite and representative of the Polarians is ended," declared the explorer, a little bitterly. " Those who received me with acclamations yesterday are ready to shower curses upon me to-day !"

" Then we must fly?"

" Assuredly !"

" But whither can we go ?"

'· I will show you !"

He waved his hand in the direction of the automobile in which his companions and the Princess Rubal were seated, and assisted Alice into the vehicle, placing her father beside her. Then he seated himself beside the doctor, on the seat beside the motorman, and the vehicle rolled away at the top of its speed.

" And now to answer your question, Alice," he resumed with gentle seriousness, looking down upon his betrothed, with Infinite tenderness. "The Eagle is at our disposal!"

"The Eagle?"

"Yes," explained Andree. "It descended three days ago in the forest of Ardloe, and word was at once brought me of the occurrence!"

"Oh, joy! Then we can leave Polaria?" cried Alice.

"We can at least make the effort," replied the explorer. "After consulting the doctor and Knut, I decided to keep the presence of the balloon a secret, and have it reinflated and otherwise put in order for another voyage."

"The fact is," said the doctor, "we had realized that Polaris would cause all the airships in his Kingdom to be destroyed, and we wanted to be ready for any emergency of the kind which has really happened."

Further details were given, as the automobile sped swiftly on its way to the forest in which the balloon was hidden.

"If we can only arrive in time—before any

measures are taken to head us off!" at length sighed Alice.

" Have no fear," returned Andree. " The new King and his friends know nothing of The Eagle."

. Little more was said until the fugitives had reached their destination and alighted.

Sure enough !

In the centre of a dense pine grove, to which Andree and its companions had caused it to be taken, the balloon was tugging gently at its fastenings, all ready for a new departure.

A few minutes sufficed for the embarkation of the fugitives, and within a minute thereafter they were soaring gently into the heavens, through which the bright beams of another morning had begun streaming.

\*        \*        \*        \*        \*

Three days later, far out in the Polar Sea, the wreck of The Eagle lay practically submerged upon the edge of a vast ice-field.

Of the explorers, not a trace !

Their dreams were ended.  But behind those dreams, what realities may not have dawned! what life even! what joy! to replace what they had lost !

**THE END.**